Survey on a Shoestring

A Manual for Small-Scale Language Surveys

Summer Institute of Linguistics and
The University of Texas at Arlington
Publications in Linguistics

Publication 96

Editors

Virgil Poulter
University of Texas
at Arlington

William R. Merrifield
Summer Institute of
Linguistics

Assistant Editors

Karl A. Franklin

Marilyn Mayers

Consulting Editors

Doris A. Bartholomew
Pamela M. Bendor-Samuel
Desmond C. Derbyshire
Robert A. Dooley
Jerold A. Edmondson

Austin Hale
Robert E. Longacre
Eugene E. Loos
Kenneth L. Pike
Viola G. Waterhouse

Survey on a Shoestring
A Manual for Small-Scale Language Surveys

Frank Blair

A Publication of
The Summer Institute of Linguistics
and
The University of Texas at Arlington
1990

© 1990 by the Summer Institute of Linguistics, Inc.
Library of Congress Catalog No: 90-071834
ISBN: 0-88312-644-3

All Rights Reserved

No part of this publication may be reproduced, stored in a retrieval system, or transmitted in any form or by any means—electronic, mechanical, photocopy, recording, or otherwise—without the express permission of the Summer Institute of Linguistics, with the exception of brief excerpts in journal articles or reviews.

Cover sketch and design by Daniel Larson and Hazel Shorey

Copies of this and other publications of the Summer Institute of Linguistics may be obtained from

International Academic Bookstore
Summer Institute of Linguistics
7500 W. Camp Wisdom Rd.
Dallas, TX 75236

To Cal and Carolyn

Table of Contents

Foreword xi

Preface xiii

1 Introduction 1

   1.1 Definitions 1
   1.2 Parts of a Survey 2

2 Survey Planning 5

   2.1 Initial Research 5
   2.2 Resources 7
   2.3 Planning 11
   2.4 Summary 20

3 Dialect Areas 21

   3.1 Introduction 21
   3.2 Procedures 26
   3.3 Summary 34

4 Sampling 35

4.1 Introduction 35
4.2 Procedures 36
4.3 Summary 50

5 Bilingualism 51

5.1 Introduction 51
5.2 Social Characteristics Influencing Bilingualism 54
5.3 Bilingualism Evaluation Methods 64
5.4 Summary 65

6 Oral Proficiency Testing 67

6.1 Description 67
6.2 Procedures 68
6.3 Advantages 70
6.4 Disadvantages 70

7 Recorded Text Tests 73

7.1 Description 73
7.2 Procedures 75
7.3 Advantages 84
7.4 Disadvantages 85

8 Observation 87

8.1 Description 87
8.2 Procedures 89
8.3 Advantages 91
8.4 Disadvantages 92

9 Sentence Repetition Tests 93

9.1 Description 93
9.2 Procedures 94
9.3 Advantages 96
9.4 Disadvantages 96

10 Self-evaluation Questionnaires ... 97

- 10.1 Description ... 97
- 10.2 Procedures ... 98
- 10.3 Advantages ... 105
- 10.4 Disadvantages ... 105

11 Language Use and Language Attitudes ... 107

- 11.1 Introduction ... 107
- 11.2 Language Use ... 108
- 11.3 Language Attitudes ... 109
- 11.4 Procedures ... 110
- 11.5 Summary ... 114

Appendix I ... 117

Appendix II ... 125

References ... 129

Foreword

Conducting a language survey is generally considered a major enterprise that requires the resources of a national census or at least a well-funded research team of professionals. Resources like this are rarely available for exploring language questions only, so linguistic survey questions often have to accompany surveys conducted for other purposes. These other surveys are likely to leave out small-group languages altogether. Data on bilingualism, more often than not, must be based on self-reports of the languages respondents say they know. These responses are often colored by contemporary attitudes about which languages are considered worth knowing or the names for languages or language varieties a speaker knows. It is common for national linguistic surveys to concentrate on bilingualism involving national languages only. Furthermore, large-scale surveys rarely if ever have useful data on how well speakers know the languages they say they know.

As a result, the language information available in censuses and other large-scale surveys are often not sufficiently detailed for those interested in Bible translation or other literacy projects for speakers of small-group languages. With the publication of Frank Blair's *Survey on a Shoestring* there is a way to get better-quality, better-focussed information on bilingualism among small ethnic groups. The beauty of the manual is that Blair shows how it can be done with a minimum of personnel, time, and equipment. Following Blair's suggestions, a team of as few as two people (only one of whom requires a knowledge of survey techniques) can visit a limited number of communities in a region and return with a more accurate picture of patterns of bilingualism and language use than might be thought possible.

Well-experienced in conducting the kind of surveys he describes and knowledgeable in the field of sociolinguistics, Blair takes his readers step by step through the procedures they will need, down to the number of recording tapes that will be needed, the style of notebook to use, and how to organize the information that will go into it. The myriad of practical details he provides is quite astonishing. Readers learn how to handle portable tape recording equipment, how to construct test texts in a number of language varieties, how to decide which locations in a region to visit, and how to decide the best order in which to visit them. When the data are collected, the manual provides detailed procedures on how to tabulate and evaluate them in both qualitative and quantative terms. Investigators who do not have sophistication in statistical terminology will be grateful for the clear and concise explanations found here. Blair's explanation of the meaning and interpretation of mean and standard deviation in the context of this kind of research, in fact, is the best I have ever seen for neophytes handling statistical data.

More than an instruction booklet, Survey on a Shoestring provides invaluable background information on bilingualism and language use and attitudes. Readers learn how bilingualism develops and is maintained in different situations, and the implications of this. Several methods for testing dialect comprehensibility are described in considerable detail, along with the advantages and disadvantages of each.

This book is one of those rare resources that combines academic-style sophistication with *what-do-I-do-next* realism. I regard it as a major contribution not only for Bible translators but for the conduct of sociolinguistic surveys in general. I cannot imagine doing survey research in sociolinguistics myself, or allowing one of my students to begin a sociolinguistic survey without consulting it.

Ralph W. Fasold
March 9, 1990

Preface

> Human speech is like a cracked kettle on which we tap crude rhythms for bears to dance to, while we long to make music that will melt the stars.
>
> Gustave Flaubert
> *Madame Bovary*

A sociolinguistic survey of an ethnolinguistic community is normally a large-scale project funded by a government or a research foundation. The results are used (or ignored) by language planners as they make decisions about language choice on the national level. That such decisions should be made at the national level is, perhaps, unavoidable; but whether they have the desired effect on the local level is often uncertain. At the local level, decisions about language choice are made by a wide variety of people—parents, school teachers, business men and women, newspaper editors, religious leaders, and others.

This manual has been prepared in response to the need to train people with little background in social research methodology. It is intended to demonstrate how a sociolinguistic survey can be carried out on a small scale, without access to the sort of funding sometimes available to national language planners, hence the title Survey on a Shoestring. In providing access to some of the tools of sociolinguistic research, I hope people primarily concerned with local languages will be able to make informed decisions about language choice at the local level. The conflicting demands of various language loyalties often place inordinate pressures on people involved in language planning decisions. Carefully planned research may help defuse such pressures; the results of such projects have proved useful in enabling people to make decisions based on facts rather than opinion.

Although this manual is the result of nearly four years of fieldwork, it is by no means intended as the final word in survey methodology. Instead, I describe the techniques and procedures which I have found to be useful in the small, rural, often illiterate, communities with which I have been primarily concerned. Not all the tools described here have been useful in every survey. Procedures and techniques which are valuable in some survey situations may prove unworkable in others. A good survey takes the time to fit the tools to the situation. My own experience in sociolinguistic surveys has been confined to Asia, and I wrote the manual to describe the surveys I have done there. I trust that the approach described here will prove helpful in other regions. I would like to thank the many people who read one of the many earlier copies of this manual and took the time to provide helpful, critical comments. I am much indebted to my colleagues and co-workers; most of the material in this book was originally hammered out in discussions with them at sites distributed throughout Asia. I am particularly grateful to Dr. and Mrs. Calvin Rensch for their patience, encouragement, and guidance.

Frank Blair
Washington, D.C.
14 March 1990

1
Introduction

You can't always get what you want
But if you try sometimes, you just might find
You get what you need.

> Mick Jagger and Keith Richards
> *You Can't Always Get What You Want*

1.1 Definitions

SURVEY, as the word is used in this manual, refers to a study which attempts to uncover and present a broad overview of the linguistic and sociolinguistic facts concerning a specific ethnolinguistic community in a particular region. A COMMUNITY may be as small as one village, or it may be as large as a people-group scattered over several states and whose only apparent connecting links are that the various subgroups perceive them-selves to be part of the same ethnolinguistic community and that the languages they speak appear to have sprung from the same linguistic stock. In multilingual ethnolinguistic communities, surveys will often necessarily need to examine the relationships which exist among the various communities.

The term FIRST LANGUAGE refers to the traditional mother tongue of the community being surveyed. This may sometimes be referred to as the VERNACULAR. The term SECOND LANGUAGE refers to any of the several additional languages that the ethnolinguistic community may use; usually it refers to the most commonly used of these. MOTHER-TONGUE SPEAKERS OF THE SECOND LANGUAGE are people who use the second language of the community under study as their mother tongue; it usually refers to members of the dominant ethnolinguistic group in the region of the survey.

BILINGUALISM is used to refer to the ability to use more than one language. As a technical term INTELLIGIBILITY is used to refer to the degree of understanding a speaker of one speech variety has of a related speech variety because of the degree of the genetic relationship between the two varieties. This is sometimes referred to as INHERENT INTELLIGIBILITY. Inherent intelligibility is thought to vary directly with the degree of the genetic relationships between speech varieties. COMPREHENSION, on the other hand, refers to the degree of understanding a speaker of one speech variety has of another speech variety because of the degree of previous exposure to it. This has sometimes been referred to as ACQUIRED INTELLIGIBILITY. Comprehension is one component of bilingual ability.

Traditionally, the criterion of intelligibility has been used by linguists to distinguish between dialect and language. For example, Lehmann, referring to the Scandinavian languages, says:

> Technically such mutually intelligible forms of speech are known as dialects, and the term language is used for mutually unintelligible forms of speech (1973:33).

The concept of MUTUAL INTELLIGIBILITY is not, however, always used in a way which sufficiently distinguishes between intelligibility and comprehension. Therefore, the term DIALECT may be more clearly used to refer to speech varieties which are linguistically similar enough to be intelligible to speakers of a related variety. The term LANGUAGE, on the other hand, refers to speech varieties which are so linguistically dissimilar as to be unintelligible to speakers of related varieties.

1.2 Parts of a Survey

Surveys of the type described in this manual investigate five different kinds of linguistic and sociolinguistic phenomena: (a) linguistic similarity, (b) dialect intelligibility, (c) multilingualism (usually referred to as bilingualism), (d) domains of language use, and (e) attitudes towards the various speech varieties current in a specific ethnolinguistic community. Sociolinguistic surveys also incorporate a demographic description of a portion of the ethnolinguistic community, as the distribution of various social characteristics throughout the community is relevant to sociolinguistic phenomena.

Surveys, by their nature, tend to be descriptive rather than theoretical, although certain theoretical concerns cannot be avoided when it comes to choosing the methods of investigation to be employed in the survey. Where these theoretical concerns are of importance to the field researcher, an

Survey on a Shoestring 3

attempt is made to describe some of the issues involved. This manual, however, is primarily a document to guide researchers in the field in their investigations into the various linguistic phenomena which are relevant to their purposes. For the sake of description and analysis it is helpful to talk about a survey in terms of its component parts. In fact each part of a survey depends on the other parts and it is not possible to complete usefully any single part of a survey in isolation from all of the other parts.

Demographic description. A demographic description seeks to identify the location and population of communities consisting in whole or in part of members of the ethnolinguistic group being studied in the region where the survey is being conducted. Part of a demographic description seeks to profile the distribution of various social characteristics (e.g. age, sex, level of education, degree of contact with speakers of other languages, etc.) within a particular subset of the population. This sample usually consists of the inhabitants of one or two villages who belong to the ethnolinguistic community being studied.

Linguistic similarity. A survey seeks to determine the degree of linguistic similarity among the vocabularies used by different members of the ethnolinguistic community who say they speak the same language and yet control different regional speech varieties. If the first language of the ethnolinguistic group is related to one of the languages of wider communication used in the region of the survey, the degree of similarity between the community's first language and second language is also of interest. If the second language is a nonstandard variety of a language which has a standard variety, the degree of similarity between the nonstandard and standard varieties may also be of interest. The degree of linguistic similarity may be determined in several ways, but is usually expressed as a percentage of phonetically similar words based on a comparison of equivalent words elicited using a standard word list.

Dialect intelligibility. A survey investigates the degree of inherent intelligibility that exists between related speech varieties used as a first language in the ethnolinguistic community being studied. The procedures used are basically those described in Casad 1974. The degree of inherent intelligibility is expressed as a percentage based on the average (mean) of the scores on a simple language test. In order to verify that acquired intelligibility is not being confused with inherent intelligibility, sample size and the standard deviation are also stated. A mean score with a high standard deviation (higher than 12–15 percent) generally indicates that what is being measured is, at least in part, comprehension, not inherent intelligibility.

Bilingualism. A survey tries to ascertain the degree of bilingual ability attained by the ethnolinguistic community being studied. Several methods of evaluating bilingualism are discussed in chapter six. Bilingual ability refers to the facility with which speakers of one language are able to understand and speak a second language in a variety of domains. If the second language is a written language, then literacy is an aspect of bilingual ability.

Domains of language use and language attitudes. In a multilingual community, the domains of language use are an important factor in understanding a community's bilingual ability. A survey investigates the domains of language use in multilingual communities. Particular attention is paid to language use patterns in the domains of the home, village pursuits, and traditional activities (including informal education in traditional values), as well as to those domains which involve contact with outsiders. Attitudes towards various patterns of language use are also investigated. Patterns of language use and language attitudes often differ radically depending on whether the concern is with a spoken or written variety of the language. If one of the languages used in the ethnolinguistic community is a written one, care must be taken to adequately distinguish the varieties involved. Language use and attitudes are usually investigated by careful observation and with informally administered questionnaires.

2
Survey Planning

> Heard melodies are sweet, but those unheard
> Are sweeter
>
> John Keats
> *Ode on a Grecian Urn*

2.1 Initial Research

The first step in any survey is the initial research. Surveys are often done by people with little firsthand knowledge about the area to which they are going. Although purposes of surveyors may differ, a survey is usually done to answer the question, "What's out there?" The ability to ask such a question implies very little previous knowledge of the area on the part of the surveyor. If a person knew what was out there, there would be no need for a survey, rather, enough information would be on hand to begin whatever project the surveyor had in mind.

There are two important sources of information which should be consulted before beginning a survey. The first is the library. Talking to people from the area to be surveyed is a second important source of information. If at all possible, both should be consulted before beginning to plan a survey. Such preliminary research can save a researcher a lot of time and trouble. For example, it is disheartening to spend a couple of months and a sum of money collecting word lists from a particular area, only to later find a previously published set of similar word lists.

Much of the information collected while doing such research can be used in the introduction to a survey report. The introduction of a survey report should contain basic information on the geography of the region, including maps of the area. It should also contain a section describing relevant ethnolinguistic communities. This section of the introduction should contain a summary of relevant cultural and linguistic information, including information about the genealogical and typological classification of the languages being surveyed.

Library. Library research includes reading all sorts of documents concerning the area to be surveyed. The major focus of such research should be linguistic and anthropological descriptions of the people living in the area to be surveyed, and surrounding areas. Other works which are often of value include the reports of administrators or missionaries who have lived in the area, of travellers who have passed through the area, and newspaper accounts. The major purpose of consulting previously written works is to inform the researcher as much as possible about the situation which prevails in the area to be surveyed.

It is important to keep track of the relevant bibliographic information for each written source consulted. An ANNOTATED BIBLIOGRAPHY is a good way to keep track of both the sources consulted and the information gleaned from them. Such a bibliography includes the title and date of publication, as well as the author's full name, name of the publisher, and the place of publication. In the case of an article, both the article title and the name of the periodical in which it was published are important.

In addition to the basic bibliographic information, an annotated bibliography contains a couple of paragraphs of comments on the document. One of these paragraphs gives a summary of the author's point of view. This paragraph includes a description of the scope of the publication and the author's findings. Another paragraph summarizes the points that the researcher finds to be particularly relevant. This paragraph frequently contains the researcher's assessment of the usefulness and reliability of the information contained in the publication.

Scholarly publications usually include bibliographies. Always examine these closely for other titles that concern the area where the survey is planned and make a note of them. Even if it is not immediately possible to obtain the publication, include it in the bibliography with a note that the document has not been personally examined. It may be that someone reading the report has access to the particular source. It is a good idea to make the bibliography as comprehensive as possible.

Bibliographic information is not the only kind of information which should be extracted from the various written sources consulted. A survey report often includes a discussion of the findings of people who have previously worked in the area to be surveyed. It is a good idea to copy or paraphrase those passages in the work which seem to summarize the author's opinion on the topics which have the most relevance to the researcher's area of interest. These QUOTATIONS are kept together with the bibliographic information until such time as they are needed for insertion into the report, with the appropriate reference to the original source.

A MAP of the area to be surveyed is an important tool for planning a survey. If at all possible obtain one before beginning data collection. Government offices, university libraries, and bookstores in larger cities are potential sources of supply. In many survey situations a map of the area will be unobtainable in the area itself—after all, the people living there already know the important points of reference.

Interviews. A second source of information which should be consulted before a survey begins is available through talking to people from the area to be surveyed. Interviewing such people can yield extremely practical information concerning life and travel in the target area. Information about modes of travel, roads and terrain, population centers, customs, diet, and social groupings are of both practical and theoretical interest to the surveyor. Often the only source of current information on some of these topics is someone from the area. If at all possible, a researcher should talk to people who know the target area before planning a survey. For example, current information about the sowing and harvesting cycles of an agricultural community is rarely available in published form. Such information is almost always best checked with someone from the area to be surveyed. Knowing when people are likely to be involved in sowing or in the harvest enables a researcher to avoid scheduling a survey for a time of the year when people are too involved in other activities to help with the research.

2.2 Resources

While the initial research into an area to be surveyed is underway, a researcher should also begin to gather the resources needed to complete the survey. Resources fall into four categories—money, equipment, personnel, and time. The amount of money, equipment, personnel, and time needed will also vary from area to area. It will also depend on the kind of survey being done. In the following discussion it is assumed that the survey includes investigations into dialect areas, bilingualism, and language use and attitudes.

Monetary. Monetary expenditures while on survey usually fall into one of three categories—travel, food, or lodging. These will vary widely from survey to survey and information about current costs can best be gathered by talking to people from the area to be surveyed. Minor equipment expenditures are often made in the course of a survey, usually for items like batteries, notebooks, and pencils. In some surveys it has occasionally been necessary to pay people for language data, but this has not been a general practice when the role of the researcher in the community is that of a 'friend of a friend'. On the whole, it is not a good idea to exchange cash payments for survey data. Once such payments are expected, the amount demanded tends to escalate and even the most casual information sharing can dry up in the absence of payment. The practice of paying for survey data can also lessen the reliability of the data collected because the people being paid to provide the data may feel more pressure to tell the researcher what they think the researcher wants to hear. Rather than paying for survey data, it may in some circumstances be helpful to hire a local assistant who can facilitate the survey over a longer period of time, conducting interviews and encouraging the participation of others.

Personnel. Perhaps the most important resource involved in any survey is personnel. The number of people involved in a survey will vary from project to project; but regardless of the number of people working on a project, there are two roles which must be filled in order for a team to be effective. People filling the role of TECHNICAL SPECIALIST or TECHNICIAN need to have a general understanding of the principles and methodology that underlie this sort of social research and know how to apply the various survey techniques. People filling the other role, that of REGIONAL SPECIALIST, need to have a knowledge of the area to be surveyed and be able to speak a variety of the language(s) to be surveyed. The person filling the role of regional specialist is sometimes referred to as the LINGUIST because of the fact that the role demands a knowledge of local languages. In some surveys the regional specialist may be from the area to be surveyed and this works very well if the regional and technical specialists are able to communicate adequately. In other cases it may be sufficient if the person filling the role of regional specialist has lived in the area to be surveyed and has gained an adequate knowledge of a variety of the local languages.

Various permutations on this basic combination of regional specialist and technician are possible. In some surveys the regional specialist and the technician may be the same person. This is normally possible only in survey situations where it is possible for the researcher to live in the ethnolinguistic community for an extended period of time. In other surveys, the role of regional specialist may be divided between two people. One of these might be a member of the local network in the area to be surveyed while the other is outsider who possesses some of the other skills needed by the survey team. For example, it sometimes happens that the technician cannot adequately communicate with a person from the area to be surveyed who would otherwise be ideal in the role of a regional specialist. In cases like this a third person who is able to communicate with the technician takes on some of the functions of the regional specialist and the local person takes the other functions.

In some surveys personnel requirements other than those intrinsic to the roles of technical and regional specialist may be important in order to ensure that data can be collected from all segments of the ethnolinguistic community. For example, in some very conservative communities, a survey team may need to be composed of both men and women so that men are available to carry out the survey among the men of the community, while women do the research among the women of the community.

Survey skills include eliciting word lists, testing intelligibility, the use of questionnaires, and other skills.

An important part of many sociolinguistic surveys is the collection of word lists. The survey team must have the ability to reliably elicit and record word lists. Usually the regional specialist is responsible for eliciting the word list and the technician is responsible for writing it down. This means that the regional specialist must have a thorough understanding of the words on the word list and be able to distinguish them from near synonyms. The regional specialist must also be able to communicate this understanding to the person from whom the responses are being elicited. The person responsible for writing down responses needs to be able to use a standard system of phonetic transcription, such as the International Phonetic Alphabet (IPA) and be able to accurately distinguish the various sounds in the speech of the person from whom a word list is being elicited. If the regional specialist has the ability to record responses phonetically, then it is preferable that s/he write down the word list. Otherwise the task falls to the technician. If it is decided to put the word list on tape, it is the technician's responsibility to obtain an adequate recording.

Procedures for creating and testing dialect intelligibility tests are described in Casad 1974. It is usually the role of the regional specialist to elicit an adequate text and the role of the technician to record it on tape. The regional specialist is usually responsible for the transcription and translation of the text and the technician for developing questions for it. It is very common, however, for both technician and regional specialist to cooperate in each of these tasks. While testing recorded texts, the regional specialist generally writes down a subject's answers and the technician controls the tape recorder. Again, it is not unusual for these roles to be shared.

Questionnaires used in a survey are usually developed initially by the technician and then modified in consultation with the regional specialist. The regional specialist generally is the person who administers the questionnaire to subjects.

A variety of methods are available for evaluating bilingualism. It is the technician's responsibility to know how to use the methods selected for the survey and to ensure that they are used appropriately. It is often the regional specialist's responsibility to actually perform the procedure with the various subjects.

Observation skills are discussed in a later section. Pertinent observations may made be either by the regional specialist or the technician, but a written record of observations should be available to the technician by the end of the survey.

The technician is usually responsible for writing up survey results. The task of organizing and analyzing the data accumulated in the course of the survey usually also falls to the technician.

Time. The amount of time needed to complete a survey depends upon the scope of the survey, the nature of the geographic area, the number of ethnolinguistic groups, and the size of the survey team. As a very general rule of thumb, it takes about three months for an experienced team of two people to survey a single ethnolinguistic community in a single district, where a district is an area that can be traversed in two days time. This allows a month for the collection of word lists and texts from different points throughout the district, a month for dialect intelligibility testing at some of those same points, and a month for a more detailed study of bilingualism, language use, and language attitudes at one or two selected points. Doubling the number of people involved in the survey does not usually halve the amount of time the survey takes, although it will be completed appreciably quicker. Nor does doubling the number of ethnolinguistic groups to be surveyed in a single district double the amount of time it takes to complete a survey, although such a survey does take longer.

Equipment. Equipment needs vary according to the type of survey being conducted. The following list of equipment is a typical field kit for a survey which involves a study of dialect areas, bilingualism, language use, and language attitudes.

1. two tape recorders (preferably with noise reduction circuits; one of these may be a tape player only)
2. microphone (preferably unidirectional)

3. patch cord (suitable for dubbing from one tape recorder to the other)
4. four–six headphones
5. Y-adapters (suitable for plugging more than one headphone into a single headphone jack)
6. two battery boxes (voltage should match that of the tape recorders)
7. five–ten sixty-minute tapes
8. spare batteries
9. copies of the word list and any questionnaires to be used
10. small notebooks, pens, pencils

2.3 Planning

The first step in planning a survey is deciding what information should be collected. Once the kind of information needed has been determined, it is possible to set goals for gathering relevant data. The goals of a survey should not be confused with its purpose. Purposes vary widely. A researcher may be collecting information for a doctoral dissertation or to decide which language is best for a functional literacy project. Goals for a survey, on the other hand, are clear statements of what the researcher intends to find out. As such, a statement of goals should briefly specify which region(s) and ethnolinguistic communities are relevant to the study, the kinds of data the survey intends to elicit and why each kind is expected to be significant, and the methods that will be used to elicit the data.

Many surveys include goals in several areas. A survey often attempts to discover the geographical distribution of the language communities as well as to delineate the different dialect areas among these communities and to discover the degree of comprehension between speakers of different dialects. In communities where some knowledge of a second language is widespread, a survey may try to ascertain the level and extent of bilingual ability, particularly if the second language is a standard language with an already existing literature. A survey may also investigate patterns of language use in the community and attitudes toward the speech varieties controlled by the community.

Statements of goals should be specific. It is not enough, for example, for a goal to be stated merely as: "to investigate multilingualism in district X." This statement is too general. It is much better to formulate statements of goals like "to find out the extent to which members of community Y in district X control Language A, as stated in SLOPE levels."

A statement like "to discover the best language for a functional literacy project" confuses purpose with goal. It is much better to state goals precisely, as in "to find out in which domains languages A and B are used by members of the Y community in district X."

Writing a statement of goals is the first part of planning any survey. It should consist of paragraphs which answer questions like the following:

1. What is the scope of the survey?
2. What regions will be included in the survey?
3. What ethnolinguistic groups are to be included in the survey?
4. What kinds of data are to be sought?
5. How will the data be elicited?

The statement of goals should be inclusive. A goal like "to discover the degree of linguistic similarity among dialects spoken in region X" should be broken down into smaller, more specific goals. For example:

1. To collect the standard 210-item word list from speakers of each of the dialects in region X.
2. To do dialect intelligibility testing among the various dialects spoken in region X using the methods described in Casad 1974.

Note that a goal statement is not the place to describe the methodology in detail, but it should mention what methods will be used.

This statement of goals actually forms the first draft of the second chapter of the final report (cf. the outline in chapter eight). In a very real way, a survey begins as well as ends with the writing of a report. A researcher should, however, be prepared to modify the goal statement as a project proceeds. Survey conditions rarely match those anticipated by the researcher in the planning stages. A statement of goals may mention only an investigation into the degree of bilingualism on the part of any particular community in the national language. In the course of a survey it may be found that one local dialect also serves as a local trade language and that the degree to which a community is bilingual in that dialect also needs to be investigated. The statement of goals will have to be modified accordingly, but it is necessary to have well-defined goals before the survey begins.

Methodology. Once the goals of a survey have been determined, it is time to decide how to reach those goals. The second step in planning a survey is to write out a description of the methods to be used in meeting the survey goals. Just as every survey report needs a statement of goals, so also it needs a description of the methodology that has been used. Such a methodology section not only describes the methods which will be used in the course of the survey, it also specifies what analytical procedures will be used and the terms in which the data will be expressed. A preliminary methodology section should be written before the survey begins to serve as a guide to procedures to be used in the survey. This forms a first draft of the third chapter of the survey report (cf. the outline in chapter eight). As is the case with the statement of goals, modifications are often made to the methodology section in the course of the survey. These modifications should be noted and incorporated into the final draft of the methodology section which is included with the final report.

If the goal statement has mentioned discovering the degree of linguistic similarity as one of the goals, then the description of methodology should indicate how the data are to be collected, how linguistic similarity will be determined, and how the data are to be expressed. A copy of the word list used is to be included in the final report, along with the data elicited using the word list. These are usually best included in an appendix, rather than incorporated directly into the methodology section.

Similarly, if the degree of intelligibility between two dialects is one of the goals of the survey, then the section which describes the methodology should indicate how intelligibility is to be investigated and how the results of analysis will be indicated. The standard procedure is described in Casad 1974, and reference should be made to that book. It is not recommended that departures be made from the techniques described there. It sometimes happens, in the course of a survey, however, that differences crop up between what the book describes and what is actually done in the field. These differences should be described in the methodology section. A copy of the texts and the questions used in dialect intelligibility testing as well as the data generated by people's responses to the texts should be placed in an appendix.

If an investigation into the degree of bilingualism is one of the goals of the survey then the methodology section should include a description of the methods used and how the results are to be expressed. If a questionnaire is used, then a copy of the questionnaire should be included in an appendix along with the data collected during the bilingualism study. Since the methodology for studies of language use and language attitudes often involves the use of questionnaires, the same would be done in these cases also.

Reference points. The first two steps in planning a survey consist of deciding what to investigate and how to investigate it. The third step consists of deciding in which locations to begin the survey. Surveys generally cover a wide enough area that it is impractical to study every hamlet in the region. Rather, a few locations are chosen and the results obtained from these few are compared with one another. These few locations are called reference points. Casad (1974:3-8) contains a helpful discussion on the selection of reference points for the purposes of dialect intelligibility studies; this discussion is intended to be somewhat more general.

The selection of reference points is best left until the researcher has had a chance to visit the region to be surveyed, or, at the very least, has had a chance to talk with people who know the region. At least three factors should be taken into account when selecting reference points—geography, contacts, and known dialect distribution.

Reference points should be selected so that they extend throughout the geographical region to be surveyed. As a rule of thumb, one reference point should be located close to the center of the area to be surveyed and others should be located at the extremities. Certain geographic features (e.g. high mountains, large bodies of water, etc.) are sometimes responsible for a greater degree of differentiation among the dialects being surveyed and care should be taken to place reference points in geographically separated spots.

As a practical matter, it is often difficult to do a survey in an area where the researcher is a completely unknown person. People all over the world are often suspicious of strangers. Such suspicion can render the process of data collection an extremely frustrating and painful affair. It will also reduce the reliability of some types of data. For these reasons it is usually a good idea to select reference points for which letters of introduction can be arranged or where the researcher can be introduced as the 'friend of a friend'. If used carefully, such a criterion for the selection of reference points need not cause the list of reference points to be unrepresentative.

Reference points should also be selected so that at least one reference point exists in each known or suspected dialect area in the region covered by the survey. Often, in the course of preliminary research or conversations with people from the area to be surveyed, evidence is discovered for the existence of different dialect areas. A common strategy involves asking speakers of one dialect whether neighboring communities speak the same, nearly the same, or quite different than they themselves do. The information gained is often quite useful when corroborated with evidence from other sources. If the criteria mentioned previously have not already located a reference point in an area where it is thought that a unique dialect may be spoken, then a new reference point should be added to the list.

These are the most common criteria for the selection of reference points. Other criteria are also possible. The importance of these criteria and the addition of others will vary from survey to survey. The list of reference points will rarely remain constant throughout a survey. It sometimes becomes apparent very early in the survey that two reference points use the same dialect and one of them may be dropped from the list. In the course of the survey evidence for the existence of previously unsuspected dialects not infrequently comes to light. If this occurs then reference points may have to be added to the list.

Common survey environments. Another factor which affects how a survey is planned and carried out is the linguistic and geographic environment of the region to be surveyed. The linguistic environment has the most effect on the kind of survey to be done and what sort of tests will be used. The geographic environment has the most effect on the practicalities of planning survey journeys—the mode of travel and the order in which reference points are to be visited. Enough information about the geographic and linguistic environment of the area to be surveyed can usually be gathered during the preliminary research stage to allow for initial planning. When the researcher arrives in the field these plans can then be refined as more information becomes available.

The linguistic environment is the complex network of interrelationships that typically exists among speech varieties used in the area to be surveyed. This discussion covers several types of linguistic environments commonly encountered on survey. It treats each environment separately, although in actual practice the different environments may overlap or combine in various ways.

In the first case, the major speech varieties in the area of a survey are so linguistically dissimilar that they cannot be considered to be part of the same language. If this fact was not clear from the information gathered while doing preliminary research, it usually becomes apparent very early in the course of the field research. As a rule of thumb, if any two word lists are less than sixty percent similar, the two varieties represented in those word lists are best thought of as separate languages or, sometimes, as very dissimilar dialects. This means that intelligibility testing need not be carried out between those two varieties. Intelligibility testing may be omitted, however, only if varieties have been shown to be very dissimilar using word lists.

In the second instance, the speech varieties used in the region of the survey cannot be considered linguistically dissimilar enough to warrant saying they are distinct languages. This seems to be one of the most common of the linguistic environments encountered on survey. As a rule of thumb, if any two word lists are more than sixty percent similar, then linguistic similarity alone is not sufficient to determine whether or not the two varieties represented in those word lists are different dialects of the same language or different languages. When this environment occurs, dialect intelligibility testing must be done to distinguish intelligibility boundaries between speech varieties. When intelligibility testing has established that several varieties are not inherently intelligible, the different varieties are often referred to as different languages. When intelligibility testing has demonstrated that several varieties are inherently intelligible, the different varieties are often referred to as different dialects of the same language.

If several varieties have been shown to be distinct languages, whether this distinction has been made on the basis of linguistic similarity or on the basis of inherent intelligibility, it is necessary to ascertain the degree of bilingualism, the language use situation, and attitudes towards the various other speech varieties independently for each language. If several speech varieties have been shown to be different dialects of the same language, and are therefore inherently intelligible, such studies need only to be done for each cluster of related dialects.

In many surveys one or more of the speech varieties used in the region may be classified as a standard variety. A standard variety of a language is often the one which has an established orthography and is taught in schools throughout the region. The standard variety is often referred to as the standard language.

If there is a standard variety of a language in the region, it is likely that there are also several nonstandard varieties. Nonstandard varieties may be distributed either geographically, socially, or according to domain (diglossia). People who control the standard variety as their mother tongue may or may not also control one or more of the nonstandard varieties. People who control a nonstandard variety as their mother tongue may or may not also control either the standard variety or other nonstandard varieties. A standard variety may or may not have mother-tongue speakers in any given region. Nonstandard varieties of a language may or may not be inherently intelligible with each other or with the standard variety. They are usually linguistically similar enough that they may be considered related languages. Nonstandard varieties which are inherently intelligible with the standard variety are sometimes referred to as nonstandard regional dialects. Nonstandard varieties which are not inherently intelligible with the standard variety are sometimes referred to as nonstandard regional languages. Whether or not a speech variety is considered a nonstandard variety of a standard language often has more to do with the community's perception of the two varieties than the degree of intelligibility which exists between them.

If the nonstandard varieties spoken in a region have mother-tongue speakers then the degree of intelligibility which exists among them must be ascertained. The degree of intelligibility between each nonstandard variety and the standard variety must also be ascertained. Care must be taken to distinguish between inherent intelligibility and comprehension (bilingualism) when testing a standard variety among various nonstandard varieties. If a dialect intelligibility test of a standard variety among mother-tongue speakers of a nonstandard variety has a standard deviation over twelve percent, it is most probable that some form of acquired intelligibility is influencing the scores. (A low standard deviation does not, however, necessarily guarantee that comprehension is not a factor.) If the mean score on the dialect intelligibility test is over eighty percent an extensive investigation into bilingualism needs to be carried out.

Bilingualism investigations are usually done with reference to the standard variety of a language. In some surveys there is not a well-defined standard variety. In cases like this, the investigation is usually done with reference to the nonstandard variety which has the largest number of mother-tongue speakers.

The linguistic environments encountered on survey often involve a combination of two or more of the environments described. For example, in a valley in the northeastern portion of the state of Maharashtra, in India, the regional language is a variety of Hindi. (Hindi is the national language of India as well as the official language of the state of Madhya Pradesh, which is the state to the immediate north of Maharashtra.) The various ethnolinguistic communities in the valley use this variety of Hindi for intergroup communication. Marathi, however, is the official language of the state of Maharashtra and this language is therefore the standard language of the valley. Schools are taught in Marathi, and it is the language used for government business. Other speech varieties used in the valley include several Indo-Aryan dialects which are linguistically similar to each other as well as to Marathi and Hindi; a Dravidian language genetically unrelated to anything else in the region; and two Munda dialects which although linguistically similar to each other, are genetically unrelated to either the Dravidian or Indo-Aryan language families.

As languages from three different linguistic families (Dravidian, Munda, and Indo-Aryan) are spoken in the valley, at one level this situation presents a linguistic environment consisting of several dissimilar speech varieties. On another level, this environment overlaps with a network of Indo-Aryan dialects and languages which compose a linguistic environment consisting of several similar varieties. Intersecting both of these is the environment which consists of the two similar Munda dialects. Superimposed over all of this is a linguistic environment which is defined by the presence of standard Marathi and of a variety of Hindi.

Just as the type of linguistic environments in which a survey is carried out affect the planning, so also the GEOGRAPHICAL ENVIRONMENT is important. The features of geography most important to survey planning are the location of the reference points in relation to each other, and the possible modes of travel between the reference points. These two factors will have a great deal of influence in determining how long a survey will take. Many surveys require more than one visit to some of the reference points. Depending on the geographic environment there are three basic sequences in which the reference points may be visited. As with the various linguistic environments, it is not uncommon for these geographic environments to overlap.

The simplest of all sequences occurs when the reference points may be ordered LINEARLY. Figure (1) assumes four such reference points: A, B, C, D. The initial reference point, A, may be the place where the researcher is residing for the duration of the survey, or it may be a convenient starting point for some other reason.

(1)   A → B → C → D → C → B → A

When the reference points can be sequenced linearly, the initial objectives of the survey (e.g., collecting texts for intelligibility testing) may be accomplished on the way up the sequence (from A to D). At D, the last reference point in the sequence, it is possible to both collect a text as well as test the texts from A, B, C, and D. Then, on the way back down the sequence (from D to A), the researcher is able to complete the testing at C, B, and A with the texts collected on the way up.

A linear sequence of reference points is very common in mountainous areas, where communities may be found along the floor of a long and relatively narrow valley. The initial point would be at the mouth of the valley. The researcher travels up the valley until the last community in the valley is reached. Along the way word lists are collected and checked, and texts are recorded and pilot tested. At the final reference point, the researcher collects the word list and text and then proceeds to test the texts collected at points A, B, and C. The researcher then turns around and returns following the same path. On the way back the various texts are tested at the various reference points. Although linear sequences of reference points commonly occur in mountain surveys, they also occur in other geographic environments.

A linear sequence of reference points is very efficient in that it allows for several objectives to be accomplished in a single round trip. Linear sequences require that a good deal of the preliminary analysis be done in the field. Linear sequences also usually require the researcher to be out in the field for an extended period of time. Depending on the temperament and other commitments of the researcher this can be either an advantage or a disadvantage.

Survey on a Shoestring

In some surveys the reference points form a LOOP. The first point on the loop, A, may be the place where the researcher is residing for the duration of the survey, or it may be a convenient place to start for other reasons. Figure (2) illustrates reference points in a loop sequence.

(2)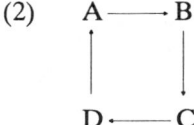

A loop sequence of reference points is very similar to a linear sequence. The only difference is that in a loop sequence the initial reference point, A, and the final reference point, D, lie close enough to each other that the researcher is able to travel from D to A without travelling through the intermediate points.

When surveying reference points in a loop sequence, the researcher travels through the sequence of reference points on the first journey as described for the linear sequence. When the final point is reached, however, the researcher returns directly to the initial point rather going through the list in reverse order.[1]

When they occur, loop sequences are often found to be more convenient than linear sequences, especially if the researcher is residing at the survey's initial reference point. Loop sequences more easily allow the researcher to do the preliminary analysis necessary between first and second journeys.

In many surveys the researcher, for one reason or another, is not able to reside at one of the reference points, but at some other location, X. This usually gives rise to visiting the reference points in a sequence like that shown in (3).

(3)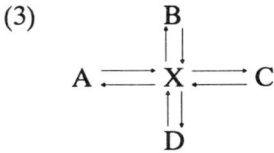

---

[1] It is of course possible for the researcher to go through reference points in a loop sequence as though it were a linear sequence, if the researcher so desires. Any loop sequence may be a linear sequence, but not all linear sequences may be loop sequences.

Centered sequences of reference points also are likely to occur if a set of reference points are approximately equidistant from any one reference point. The central point, X, may or may not be a reference point, but because of the exigencies of the survey, the researcher finds it necessary to return to 'home base' after a visit to each reference point.

Centered sequences are not the most efficient of the possible sequences. They usually require a great deal more time to be spent travelling. On the other hand, they drastically reduce the amount of time that a researcher needs to spend away from 'home base' at a stretch.

2.4 Summary

This section has looked at the various factors which must be taken into account when planning a survey. The first step in any survey is the preliminary research. Then the researcher needs to decide what kind of survey to do and to take stock of the resources available for the survey. When the goals, methodology and probable time-frame of a survey have been decided upon, research can begin. A set of objectives for a typical survey has been discussed. As surveys must also take into account the linguistic and geographical environment of the region where they take place, frequently encountered environments were discussed.

3
Dialect Areas

I now for the first time realized the difficulty of obtaining precise information from uneducated people with regard to their language. In particular, it was most difficult to get them to give me the different parts of verbs. I would ask, for example, "How would you say, 'I am ill?'" They gave me a sentence which I wrote down. Then I asked, "Now, what is 'thou art ill?'" They repeated the same sentence. "That can't be right," I said. "They can't both be the same." "Yes, that is right," they answered. "If we want to say 'Thou art ill,' we say just what we have told you." "Well, but suppose you were ill yourself what would you say?" "Oh, then we should say so-and-so." This readiness in misapprehending one's meaning and reversing what one has said gave rise to one class of difficulties. Another class rose from the extreme simplicity of the people. For instance, after asking them the words for a number of common objects in their language, I asked, "And what do you call 'city?'" "*Káshán*," they replied. "Nonsense!" I said "*Káshán* is the name of a particular city. What do you call cities in general?" "No," they said, "It is quite right. In Persian you say '*shahr mi-ravam*,' 'I am going to the city'. We say '*Káshán mi-ravam*'. It is all the same." It was useless to argue or to point out that there were many other cities in the world besides *Káshán*. To these folk *Káshán* remained 'the city' par excellence, and they could not see what one wanted with any other. Finally I had to give up the struggle in despair, and to this day I do not know whether the *Kohrúdí* dialect possesses a general term for 'city' or not.

Edward Granville Brown, 1893
A Year among the Persians

3.1 Introduction

A common goal of many surveys is to discover the geographical distribution of communities using different speech varieties in the region being surveyed. A survey does this by determining the degree of linguistic similarity among the geographically distributed communities and by ascertaining the level of intelligibility which exists among them. This part of a survey is an investigation into dialect areas. Such an investigation is usually carried out on the first two survey journeys.

Dialect chains and dialect networks. A central finding of comparative linguistics is that the degree of difference between two speech communities often increases as distance between them increases. As the Punjabi proverb has it, "The water changes every five miles, and the dialect every two." Such dialect variation is sometimes thought of as abrupt, as though speech varieties were akin to nationality and that by crossing an invisible border a great change is wrought. It is much more often the case that speech varieties differentiate gradually and slowly over distance. When a string of dialects is marked by small differences between nearby dialects but by greater differences between dialects at the ends of the string, linguists speak of such a string of geographical dialects as a DIALECT CHAIN. Bailey (1908) describes a dialect chain in what is now the state of Himachal Pradesh in India in terms of the

> ... gradual changes by which a dialect merges into the one geographically next to it. This is amply exemplified in the chain of dialects from Simla via Kulu or Mandi to the Banihal Pass or Kishtawar.

The dialect of Simla is perceived as shading into the dialect of Mandi, which is perceived as shading into the dialect of Kishtawar, and so on. Figure (4) illustrates this relationship.

(4)   Simla ⟵⟶ Mandi ⟵⟶ Kishtawar

The differentiation of speech varieties, however, does not always occur in a linear fashion. Such changes in speech varieties are often multidirectional, which can make it very difficult to isolate a single variety as though it were a point on a continuum. In cases like this linguists speak of DIALECT NETWORKS. A dialect network is more than a set of interconnected points on a continuum. The relationship between different speech varieties can become quite complicated. Saussure describes the situation as:

> The current practice, which differs from ours, is to picture dialects as perfectly defined linguistic types, bounded in all directions and covering distinct zones placed side by side on a map (a, b, c, d, etc.). But natural dialect transformations produce entirely different results. As soon as we studied each phenomenon separately and determined its spread, our old notion had to give way to the new one: there are only natural dialectal features, not natural dialects; in other words, there are as many dialects as there are localities (1959:201).

Survey on a Shoestring 23

Figure (5) is similar to one Saussure used to illustrate his point.

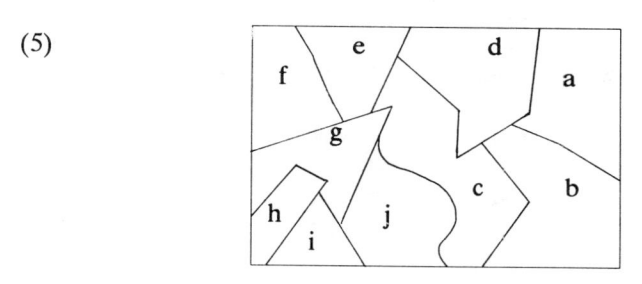

(5)

And yet, the identification of different dialect areas, whether they comprise dialect chains or dialect networks, is one of the goals of most surveys. Different dialect areas are typically distinguished by the results of word list comparison and dialect intelligibility testing. Three possible combinations of results are relevant. Figure (6) summarizes these. Word lists and dialect intelligibility testing are used together to distinguish different dialect areas. One technique provides something the other lacks. Word lists provide information about the linguistic relationships between speech varieties insofar as these relationships are not blurred by borrowing. Dialect intelligibility tests help delineate the existing intelligibility networks. Both are necessary for a clear understanding of the situation in the region being surveyed.

(6) Percentage of Similar Words

Inherent Intelligibility	Above 60%	Below 60%
Above 80%	Several very similar speech varieties may be referred to as similar dialects if inherent intelligibility is high.	Several dissimilar or slightly similar speech varieties may be referred to as different languages. (No dialect intelligibility testing is required.)
Below 80%	Several very similar speech varieties may be referred to either as dissimilar dialects or different languages if inherent intelligibility is low.	

If the results of a word list comparison show greater than sixty percent similarity between two speech varieties, dialect intelligibility testing must be done. If the results show less than eighty percent intelligibility, the speech varieties are referred to as either 'dissimilar dialects' or 'different languages', according to the conventions governing the use of the terms 'dialect' and 'language' in the area being surveyed. If the results of dialect intelligibility testing show that intelligibility is high, then the speech varieties may be referred to as 'similar dialects'.

If word lists are less than sixty percent similar, then the speech varieties are referred to as 'different languages'. As a rule of thumb, no dialect intelligibility testing need be done between different languages.[2]

A surveyor should be careful about saying that two speech varieties represent the 'same' dialect or language. Whether or not two speech varieties are identical is a judgment that is nearly impossible for an outsider to make on the basis of the limited sort of data collected on a survey. Such a judgment depends a lot on the perceptions of mother-tongue speakers of the speech varieties involved. These perceptions are usually unavailable to a surveyor without (at the very least) a thorough language attitude study. Fortunately, discovering whether or not two speech varieties may be considered to be similar dialects is sufficient for the purposes of most surveys.

Inherent intelligibility and acquired intelligibility. Note that (6) refers to inherent intelligibility. Inherent intelligibility is the degree of understanding which a speakers of one dialect have of a similar dialect because the two dialects spring from the same linguistic stock. Inherent intelligibility may be contrasted with acquired intelligibility. Acquired intelligibility is the degree of understanding speakers of one speech variety have of another speech variety, which may or may not be linguistically related, because of their exposure to it. Generally speaking, the degree of inherent intelligibility is constant throughout a community, while the degree of acquired intelligibility will vary according to the degree of exposure to the second speech variety that different segments of the community

---

[2]It may be necessary, however, to test for acquired intelligibility (i.e., bilingualism) in such situations. Although recorded text testing may be used to test for acquired intelligibility as well as inherent intelligibility, the sampling procedure is quite different and the use of such tests for bilingualism is discussed in the relevant chapter. It is possible to conduct pilot tests of bilingual ability on a small sample using recorded text tests at the same time dialect intelligibility testing is being done, but it must be realized that such results are not definitive with regard to acquired intelligibility.

have had. A community is homogeneous with regard to inherent intelligibility; it is usually heterogeneous with regard to acquired intelligibility.

The fact that a community is expected to be homogeneous with regard to inherent intelligibility makes it fairly easy to tell if the results of recorded text tests are indicative of the degree of inherent intelligibility. Figure (7) summarizes the relationship between standard deviation and the average score on a dialect intelligibility test.

(7)

	Standard Deviation	
Average Score	High	Low
High	Situation 1 Many people understand the story on the test tape well, but some have difficulty.	Situation 2 Most people understand the story on the test tape.
Low	Situation 3 Many people cannot understand the story, but a few are able to answer correctly.	Situation 4 Few people are able to understand the story on the test tape.

For most purposes, a score above eighty percent on a recorded text test is considered to be high; low scores are those below sixty percent. A standard deviation is considered high if it is greater than twelve to fifteen percent. It is low if it is less than ten to twelve percent. As a rule of thumb, if the standard deviation of a set of scores from dialect intelligibility tests is low (as in situations two and four), then the scores are probably an indication of inherent intelligibility. If the standard deviation is high (as in situations one and three) then what is being measured is at least partly acquired intelligibility. A high standard deviation on a recorded test text is a finding no less valuable than a low standard deviation, for it is often the first clue pointing towards the existence of acquired intelligibility. Such a finding sometimes indicates the need for a more thorough bilingualism study with reference to the dialects concerned.

It is important to note that interpreting data derived from dialect intelligibility tests in this fashion is only appropriate if adequate care has been taken to ensure that the small sample tested for dialect intelligibility includes a diversity of social characteristics (e.g., age, education, sex, etc.) among the people tested. If the sample is not sufficiently diverse, standard deviation is not a reliable guide for deciding whether the degree of intelligibility being measured is inherent or acquired. Similarly, standard deviation is not a reliable guide to the kind of intelligibility being measured if an identifiable subset of the people tested have had a similarly greater degree of exposure to the dialect being tested than other people in the sample.

Situation one may occur when the speech varieties being tested are similar dialects and the sample is sufficiently diverse. High standard deviations sometimes occur as a result of inadequately control-tested ('hometown' tested) recorded text tests or because of a difference in the degree of contact different subjects have had with the dialect being tested.

Situation two often, but not necessarily, occurs when similar dialects are being tested. The sample should be checked for sufficient diversity. This situation sometimes results when, for example, a sample consisting entirely of young men with some education is being tested in a dialect similar to the language of education. Their ability in their second language carries over into the dialect being tested resulting in a score which may not be valid for the community as a whole.

Situations three and four more often occur when different languages or dissimilar dialects are being tested. A high standard deviation in situation three is perhaps more likely to be the result of different degrees of contact with other dialects than in situation one.

3.2 Procedures

> Ye knowe ek that forme of speche is chaunge
> Withinne a thousand yer, and wordes tho
> That hidden prys now wonder nyce and straunge
> Us thinketh hem, and yet they spake hem so.
>
> Chaucer
> *Troylus and Criseyde II, 22-25*

Word lists elicited from different communities are compared and the percentage of those items determined to be similar is calculated. The level of intelligibility among the speech varieties being investigated is ascertained by means of dialect intelligibility testing. Dialect intelligibility relationships are expressed in terms of the percentage of correct answers to the questions on a recorded text test.

Survey on a Shoestring

Word Lists. The following information should be collected with each word list:

1. Language Name
2. Alternate Names
3. Location[3]
4. Recorded by
5. Date
6. Name of Speaker
7. Speaker's home village
8. Age of Speaker
9. Sex of Speaker

A sample word list, the one used for surveys in South Asia, may be found on the following pages. It is included here, not as a standard word list for all surveys everywhere, but rather as an example of a word list which has been contextualized to a particular linguistic area. This word list was constructed after pilot-testing word lists on three different surveys in South Asia. At that point, it was decided to keep this version as the standard. Were it to be revised again, items 11, 23, and 24 would probably be replaced with items less likely to have such a wide range of euphemisms. Similarly items 104, 111, and 115 have too great a degree of semantic overlap, as do items 104, 112, and 116; items 102, 105, and 113; and items 103, 106, and 114.

A word list should always be elicited from a mother-tongue speaker of the language. Care should be taken in order to ensure that the person or people from whom the word list is elicited are actually long-term residents of the area.

Always take the most generic term for an item on the word list. If no general term for a word is available, then use the name of the most common variety. For example, if no generic word for monkey exists in the language, and langurs are the most common variety of simian in the area, then take the word for langur. Make a note in parentheses that the word means langur, and not monkey. Some items on the word lists already have common varieties cited in parentheses for them. These are meant to be used as aids in choosing such common varieties, or to make clarification in cases where the sense of the English word is not clear without some context. They are not to be used if a generic word is available, only to serve as a guide if a generic word is not available. For example, some

---

[3]Note that the location should be specified as completely as possible, mentioning the village name as well as such larger entities as are appropriate, up to an including the province or state, for two reasons: (a) other people will want to use the data who are not as familiar with the area as the person who records the word list, and (b) some town or village names will occur more than once on a survey and it will be helpful to know from just which Williamsburg, Alexandria, or Santiago a particular word list came from.

Survey Word List

1. body
2. head
3. hair
4. face
5. eye
6. ear
7. nose
8. mouth
9. teeth
10. tongue
11. breast (woman's)
12. belly
13. arm
14. elbow
15. palm
16. finger
17. nail
18. leg
19. skin
20. bone
21. heart
22. blood
23. urine
24. feces
25. village
26. house
27. roof
28. door
29. firewood
30. broom
31. mortar (for grinding spice)
32. pestle (for grinding spice)
33. hammer (for breaking stone)
34. knife (for cutting meat)
35. axe (for cutting wood)
36. rope
37. thread
38. needle
39. cloth
40. ring (gold band)
41. sun
42. moon
43. sky
44. star
45. rain
46. water
47. river
48. cloud (white)
49. lightning
50. rainbow
51. wind
52. stone (fist-sized)
53. path (walking)
54. sand
55. fire
56. smoke
57. ash
58. mud (wet)
59. dust
60. gold
61. tree
62. leaf
63. root
64. thorn
65. flower
66. fruit
67. mango
68. banana
69. wheat (husked)
70. millet (husked)
71. rice (husked)
72. potato
73. eggplant
74. groundnut
75. chili (whole, red, dry)
76. turmeric
77. garlic
78. onion
79. cauliflower
80. tomato
81. cabbage
82. oil
83. salt
84. meat (raw)
85. fat
86. fish
87. chicken
88. egg
89. cow
90. buffalo
91. milk
92. horns
93. tail
94. goat
95. dog
96. snake
97. monkey
98. mosquito
99. ant
100. spider
101. name
102. man
103. woman
104. child
105. father
106. mother
107. older brother
108. younger brother
109. older sister
110. younger sister
111. son
112. daughter
113. husband
114. wife
115. boy
116. girl
117. day
118. night
119. morning
120. noon
121. evening/afternoon
122. yesterday
123. today
124. tomorrow
125. week
126. month
127. year
128. old (object)
129. new (object)
130. good
131. bad
132. wet
133. dry
134. long (object)
135. short (object)
136. hot (water)
137. cold (water)
138. right
139. left
140. near
141. far
142. big
143. small
144. heavy
145. light
146. above
147. below
148. white
149. black
150. red
151. one
152. two
153. three
154. four
155. five
156. six
157. seven
158. eight
159. nine
160. ten
161. eleven
162. twelve
163. twenty
164. one hundred
165. who?
166. what?
167. where?
168. when?

Survey on a Shoestring

169. how many?	183. bite (verb)	197. go
170. what kind?	184. be hungry	198. come
171. this (in hand)	185. drink	199. speak
172. that (distant)	186. be thirsty	200. hear
173. these (in hand)	187. sleep	201. see
174. those (distant)	188. lie down	202. I (1s)
175. same (like)	189. sit down	203. you (2s, informal)
176. different (other)	190. give	204. you (2s, formal)
177. whole (unbroken)	191. burn (wood)	205. he (3s, masculine)
178. broken (pot)	192. die	206. she (3s, feminine)
179. few	193. kill	207. we (1p, inclusive)
180. many	194. fly (bird)	208. we (1p, exclusive)
181. all	195. walk	209. you (2p)
182. eat	196. run	210. they (3p)

languages do not have a single word for 'cloud'. Instead there are two words, one for 'white cloud' and one for 'dark cloud'. The word list has 'white' in parentheses following the word 'cloud'. This means that the word for 'white cloud' should be taken, but only if there is no generic word for cloud. In the case of the words for domestic animals, it is often the case that these nouns differ according to the sex and age of the animal. If there is no generic name for the domestic animal, elicit the form used for mature female animals (e.g., cow, not bull or calf).

If adjectives are marked for gender, record the masculine form.

In the case of verbs, two forms should be elicited. One of these should be the third person masculine form of the simple past tense (e.g., 'he ran'), or its closest equivalent in the language. The second form may be the second person singular informal imperative, such as is used in giving a command to a child (e.g., '(you) go!'). If the language has more than one level of formality, elicit the command that is used to children.

All words elicited should be checked in a simple sentence which makes it clear that the right word has been elicited. This is particularly true when eliciting the first person plural inclusive and exclusive pronouns. For the first person plural inclusive pronoun it is useful to use a sentence like "We are people." This may then be contrasted with "We are ... " to elicit the first person plural exclusive pronoun, where the blank is filled with the name of the appropriate ethnolinguistic group.

The appropriate formal and informal pronouns may often be elicited by having the speaker address a child and an older male relative.

Once a word list has been elicited, it should be checked with a second set of mother-tongue speakers of the language being studied. Variants, near-synonyms, and synonyms should be discussed at this time, as they occur; and a decision should be made about which form to include in the word list.

Word lists should always be written on paper with ruled lines. A copy book is a convenient place to write word lists as it prevents loose pages from being accidentally lost and can also be used for other information on the language. The language name should be written at the top of each column of word lists. Write the English gloss on the same line as the word elicited. This ensures that the word list is useful to someone who may not have a copy of the master list. It also helps prevent mistakes caused by accidentally skipping a word.

If the word list is going to be taped, the tape should also have recorded on it all the relevant information about the language and people involved in the elicitation. The number and the English gloss should be recorded, followed by the word itself pronounced twice. Following the repetition, a short sentence containing the word may be recorded.

Analysis of word lists consists of grouping similar words together and then counting what percentage of two word lists have been grouped together. Such analysis usually involves copying the word lists over into a central file or notebook in such a way that they can be easily compared. In such a file all the words elicited by one item on the word list are arranged in a column on a single page of the file or notebook. The order of the languages to which the words belong should be the same on each page. The numeral '1' is placed by the first word in the column and by all words in the column for that gloss which are considered to be similar. The numeral '2' is placed by the next item in the column which does not have a number, and all the words similar to it. This process is repeated until all the words have a numeral by them. Once this has been done for each item on the word list, it is a relatively simple matter to go through and see how many words of any two languages belong to the same similarity groupings.

Decisions about similarity groupings may be made in several different ways. The soundest is based on the comparative method as it is used by linguists doing comparative studies. This process is often more time-consuming than a researcher on survey could desire. It also may require information not readily available to the surveyor.

Simons (1984) and Wimbish (1989) describe programs which automate much of the lexicostatistic process so that it may be done quickly on a small computer. The programs require that the researcher make the initial similarity groupings. The program then calculates the similarity percentages for each pair of word lists. This much is very useful, although in itself does not guarantee that the comparative method has been adequately applied. The programs are also capable of evaluating the various sound correspondences yielded by the word list and flagging unlikely correspondences in the similarity groupings as they have been entered by the researcher. The researcher may then alter the similarity groupings as they have been entered to bring them into accordance with the sound correspondences and then recalculate the similarity percentages. When this has been done,

Survey on a Shoestring

the percentages are much more likely to represent true cognates and may be described as cognate relationships.

Whether or not such a program is used, it is still incumbent upon the researcher to make the initial similarity groupings. Such decisions are lexicostatistical in nature, and a set of criteria for these decisions is desirable in order to ensure a degree of uniformity among the similarity percentages calculated by different researchers. The following standard has been contextualized with some success in surveys in South Asia. According to it, all pairs of phones in two words being compared are classified into one of three categories.

CATEGORY ONE includes the following possibilities:

a. Exact matches (e.g., [b] occurs in the same position in each word.)
b. Vowels which differ by only one phonological feature (e.g., [i] and [e] occur in the same position in each word.)
c. Phonetically similar segments which occur consistently in the same position in three or more word pairs. For example, the [g]/[gɦ] correspondences in the following entries from these two dialects would be considered category one:

	Dialect One	Dialect Two
fingernail	[goru]	[gɦoru]
axe	[godeli]	[gɦodel]
cloth	[guda]	[gɦuda]
boy	[peka]	[pekal]

CATEGORY TWO consists of the following:

a. Those phonetically similar nonvocalic segments which are not attested in three pairs (cf. the above example.)
b. Vowels which differ by two or more phonological features (e.g., [a] and [u]).

CATEGORY THREE includes the following possibilities:

a. All corresponding segments which are not phonetically similar.
b. A segment which corresponds to nothing in the second word of the pair. For example, the [l]/[#] correspondence in the word for 'boy' in the example above.

In contextualizing these rules to specific surveys in South Asia, the following differences between two items are ignored:

a. interconsonantal [ə],
b. word initial, word final, or intervocalic [h, ɦ],
c. any deletion which is shown to be the result of a regularly occurring process in a specific environment.

Each pair of corresponding phones in each pair of words is classified according to one of these three categories. The number of phones in a word as well as the categories to which different phones belong determines whether two words are to be considered similar. The length of a word is determined by counting the number of phones in the word. If two words have a different number of phones, the length of the longer of the two is taken. The various permissible categories of similar words are summarized in (8).

(8) Word Length and Linguistic Similarity

Word Length		Category One	Category Two	Category Three
2	=	2	0	0
3	=	2	1	0
4	=	2	1	1
5	=	3	1	1
6	=	3	2	1
7	=	4	2	1
8	=	4	2	2
9	=	5	2	2
10	=	5	3	2
11	=	6	3	2
12	=	6	3	3

In other words, if each of a pair of words has two phones, both pairs of phones have to be in category one in order for the two words to be considered similar. If each of a pair of words is three phones in length, either all the phones must be in category one or two of them must be in category one and one of them may be in category two. If each of a pair of words is four phones in length, either all of the corresponding pairs of phones must be in category one, or three pairs of phones can be in category one and one pair may be in category two or three, or two pairs of phones may be in category one and one pair of phones may be in category two and one pair in category three. These criteria set the lower threshold for similarity; a pair of words may be more similar than the criteria described here, but they may not be less similar and still be considered similar.

These guidelines are meant only as suggestions and may have to be modified some to meet the conditions of a particular survey. For example, these guidelines offer no suggestions about cases of metathesis. Some decisions will have to be made on a case by case basis. However, once a modification in the procedure is introduced, the modified procedures should be applied as extensively as possible so that the resulting calculations will be as comparable as possible.

Dialect intelligibility testing. The procedures for creating and administering recorded text tests are set forth in *Dialect Intelligibility Testing* by Eugene Casad (1974). These procedures have been used in many parts of the world and found to give fairly satisfactory results. It is strongly recommended that a researcher follow them. So-called 'shortcuts' in these procedures have an alarming tendency to yield invalid and unreliable data. Two such 'shortcuts' are particularly important to avoid. First, the recorded texts used for dialect intelligibility testing must not be translated texts. It is acceptable for someone who is literate to write out the text first and then read it, providing the language's literary variety or the person's reading style does not render this invalid. It is acceptable for the texts to be modified in accordance with suggestions from the researcher. What must be avoided is the possibility of the results of a dialect intelligibility test being based on a speech variety that has been artificially modified by the constraints invariably involved in a translation. The second 'shortcut' which must be avoided is the temptation to have the questions on the text asked in the same language as the text. The questions in a dialect intelligibility test must be asked in the mother tongue of the person being tested. A step-by-step description of the processes involved in recorded text testing is given in this manual's chapter on bilingualism.

Casad states that a control test of a recorded text test (also referred to as 'hometown' test) should have a score approximating one hundred percent. Although it seems obvious that a community should score one hundred percent on a recorded text test in its own language, for a variety of reasons this does not always occur. These reasons range from inattentiveness or unfamiliarity of the subjects with the testing technique to improperly framed questions and inadequate understanding of the text material on the part of the researchers. Casad describes early attempts to compensate for low scores on a hometown test by increasing all the scores on a particular text by the amount needed to bring the control test up to one hundred. This method of compensation is not valid and should not be used. A better practice is to discard any question which was missed more than once on the control test. As the number of questions on a recorded text test should be ten, this requires that fifteen or so questions be tested for the control test and the inadequate questions (i.e., those which have been missed more than once) be discarded. Tests which have been constructed in this way will always have a control score of higher than ninety percent. It is best to aim for a control test score of a hundred percent, but tests with control scores as low as 95 percent have been used.

Two other points about the methodology of dialect intelligibility testing should also be made here. The first is that every subject should be tested on a text in his or her own language. If the researcher does not have a score for a subject on a text in the subject's mother tongue, it is impossible for that subject's scores on other texts to be properly evaluated. As a corollary to this, it is impossible to evaluate the scores on any text of any subject who cannot score seventy percent or higher on a recorded text test in his or her mother tongue. If a subject misses four or more questions out of ten on a test in the subject's mother tongue, a test on which other speakers of the same mother tongue have scored ninety or one hundred percent, then it is likely that something is interfering with that subject's ability to take recorded text tests, and that subject's scores should not be included in the sample.

The second methodological point which should be made here is that the sample for dialect intelligibility testing, normally ten subjects, needs to be diverse. A sample for dialect intelligibility testing should include people from both sexes and a variety of age and educational levels. This is true even though inherent intelligibility is, theoretically, homogeneous throughout a community. Scores on recorded text tests cannot in themselves distinguish between acquired and inherent intelligibility. An analysis of the scores which involves calculating the standard deviation can do so, but only if the sample is sufficiently diverse.

3.3 Summary

This chapter has discussed the delineation of dialect areas in accordance with data collected using word lists and dialect intelligibility tests. Methods of assessing the degree of similarity among word lists and analyzing and interpreting the results of dialect intelligibility tests have been discussed. This chapter also briefly introduced the concepts of dialect networks and dialect chains and discussed the difference between acquired and inherent intelligibility. A method of making lexicostatistical judgments which has been found useful in surveys in South Asia was also described.

4
Sampling

A Bill for taking a census has passed the House of Representatives, and is with the Senate. It contains a schedule for ascertaining the component classes of the society, a kind of information extremely requisite to the Legislator, and much wanted for the science of Political Economy. A repetition of it every ten years would hereafter afford a most curious and instructive assemblage of facts. It was thrown out by the Senate as a waste of trouble and supplying materials for idle people to make a book.

James Madison
Letter to Thomas Jefferson
February 14, 1790

4.1 Introduction

One goal of social research is often to find correlations between a particular social characteristic, such as level of bilingualism, or a good attitude toward the second language, and any of a number of other social characteristics, such as age, sex, education, or frequency of contact with speakers of the second language.[4] In the language of social research, the characteristic being investigated is called the DEPENDENT VARIABLE. The characteristics which are thought to influence the dependent variable are called INDEPENDENT VARIABLES. The independent variables, those which correlate with the level of bilingualism or a good attitude towards the second language, vary from community to community.

Careful sampling techniques are necessary in several parts of a sociolinguistic survey. They are frequently used in studies of bilingualism, language

---

[4]Frequency of contact with speakers of a second language is often a function of other characteristics of an ethnolinguistic group, such as occupation, geographic or social distance from a population of speakers of the second language, or seasonal migration patterns.

use, and language attitudes. This discussion of sampling uses level of bilingualism as an example of a dependent variable, and those characteristics which often influence bilingualism as examples of independent variables. But the techniques discussed can be applied equally well to other investigations.

4.2 Procedures

The first step in any bilingualism study is to determine the existence and distribution of those independent variables which are likely to correlate with various levels of bilingualism in a particular community. In many communities degree of bilingual ability correlates with amount of education. In order to test such a hypothesis in a particular community, the level and distribution of education throughout the community must be known. The existence and distribution of such variables may be determined by developing a demographic profile of the community. The information in the demographic profile is collected using a community census.

Once it is known which independent variables are important, it can then be decided which people to test for bilingual ability. Most communities are too large for it to be possible to test every member for their bilingual ability. Therefore only a portion of the people in the community is tested. The portion of the community that is tested is called the SAMPLE. Fasold gives the following description of a sample:

> A sample consists of a small number of members of a population which can be studied in detail. The results can then be projected to the population as a whole. In order for this projection to be accurate, the sample should be a microcosm of the whole population... Making sure that the sample represents the population in all crucial ways is not easy (1984:86–87).

In deciding which people should be included in the sample, it is necessary to ensure that each of the independent variables included in determining the sample composition is relevant to the investigation. In one community, sex, age, and education may be the important characteristics which are thought likely to correlate with bilingual ability. The sample must then include people of both sexes, at a variety of ages, and of different educational levels. One way to ensure this is to draw a chart like that in (9), which represents the different groups in the desired sample.

In this sample, age and education are each assigned three possible VALUES. These values are selected to reflect those which occur in the population at large. The selection of values is based on the demographic

(9) A Hypothetical Sample

	Men			Women		
SCHOOL:	None	Primary	Secondary	None	Primary	Secondary
AGE (in years)						
Young (15–30)	5	5	5	5	5	5
Middle (31–45)	5	5	5	5	5	5
Older (46+)	5	5	5	5	5	5
	15 +	15 +	15 +	15 +	15 +	15 = 90

profile of the general population, which will be discussed in the next subsection. The selection of values for the variables, as well as the choice of relevant variables themselves, will not be the same for every study. For example, in a community in which there is no secondary education and for which education is a variable thought to influence bilingual ability, it may be sufficient to have only two categories—educated and noneducated. As seen in (9), this sample has eighteen cells in the matrix. For the results to have a chance at being statistically valid, an absolute MINIMUM of five people must be tested for each cell. For statistical purposes, it is much better if there are more than five people for each cell. If there are less than five, the data for that cell cannot be considered reliable. Eighteen cells, with a minimum of five people for each, yields a sample size of 90 people.

Variables and values for those variables are based upon data from the demographic profile. In any given population, however, not all possible combinations of the relevant values and variables may exist. For example, in the population for which the sample in (9) was prepared, it may happen that no one over 45 years of age has been to school, because schools were only introduced in the community forty years ago. Secondary schools were introduced only ten years ago, so no one over the age of thirty has attended secondary school. And because it is a very conservative community, it may be that very few, if any, women have attended school. If these things are true, then the sample should be adjusted to look like that in (10).

Such adjustments as these can only be made after a demographic profile has been done in order to ascertain whether the categories of people in the sample actually exist. Such adjustments should not be made on the basis of a novice's intuition or guesses about the community. As Fasold (1984:87) says, it is very difficult to ensure that a sample is adequately representative of an entire population. Doing a demographic profile and following a careful sampling technique is a way of attempting to ensure the reliability of the data. When done in this way it is easy to determine what

(10) An Adjusted Hypothetical Sample

	Men			Women		
SCHOOL:	None	Primary	Secondary	None	Primary	Secondary
AGE: (in years)						
Young (15–30)	5	5	5	5	0	0
Middle (31–45)	5	5	0	5	0	0
Older (46+)	5	0	0	5	0	0
	15 +	10 +	5 +	15 +	0 +	0 = 45

sort of people need to be tested in order to assess a population's bilingual ability. It is also easy to determine when enough people have been tested and the sample is complete.

Note that this is not the only way to create a representative sample. When testing for bilingual ability is complete, a sample done in this way will yield an average score for each cell in the matrix. This score is then compared with the demographic profile to see what portion of the population as a whole belongs to that category. If it is known that men under thirty years of age with a secondary school education have a high degree of bilingual ability, and it is known that ten percent of the population consists of men under thirty years of age with a secondary school education, then it may be concluded that at least ten percent of the population is very bilingual. A sample done in this way not only shows how bilingual a population is, it also shows the distribution of bilingual ability throughout the population.

Demographic profile. A demographic profile of a community is a summary of how various social characteristics are distributed throughout the community under investigation. A demographic profile can range in complexity from a simple two-cell matrix like that in (11) to huge databases which are best maintained on a computer.

(11) Male   Female
     49   51

From (11) it is easy to find out what percentage of the sample population is male and what percentage is female. (12) is an example of a more detailed demographic profile like those often compiled in the course of survey work.

The demographic profile in (12) records information on three social characteristics—age, sex, and education. Sex is necessarily a characteristic with

Survey on a Shoestring

only two values. Age and education have been divided into three categories each in this example. The total number of people represented in this demographic profile is 130. The numbers in each cell represent the number of people in the population for whom all three of the characteristics are true. For example, there are nine young men with no education in the population represented here. The numbers in brackets represent subtotals in various categories. For example, there are 21 older men in the population and 62 women (of all age groups). With a demographic profile organized in this manner it is relatively easy to calculate what percentage of the population belongs to various categories. For example, women represent 47.7 percent of this population, older men represent 16.2 percent, and uneducated young men represent 6.9 percent of the population. Similarly, 63.8 percent have never been to school, and only 17.7 percent of the women have been to school. A demographic profile shows the distribution of various social characteristics throughout a population.

(12) Demographic Profile of a Village Population

		Men			Women			
SCHOOL:		None	Primary	Secondary	None	Primary	Secondary	
AGE:	(in years)							
Young	(15–30)	9	7	13 [29]	19	4	7 [30]	59
Middle	(31–45)	7	2	9 [18]	20	0	0 [20]	38
Older	(46+)	16	4	1 [21]	12	0	0 [12]	33
		32	13	23 [68]	51	4	7 [62]	130

Such a distribution is useful for two reasons. As has been mentioned, it is useful in deciding which variables and which values for those variables are important in selecting a sample. It is also useful when it comes to interpreting the data on bilingualism which has been collected. The knowledge that young men with a secondary school education tend to be the most bilingual portion of a community is much more valuable if it is also known what percentage of the population may be described as young, male, and well-educated.

Collection of census data. The tool used to develop a demographic profile is a CENSUS. A census is a set of questions for which answers are gathered for every individual in a particular community. The following is a list of the different kinds of information it is useful to collect:

1. Number of Interview
2. Date of Interview
3. Location of Interview
4. Name
5. Age
6. Sex
7. Education
8. Occupation
9. Previous Occupation(s)
10. Mother Tongue
11. Other Tongue
12. Place of Current Residence
13. Duration of Current Residence
14. Place(s) of Previous Residence
15. Duration of Previous Residence
16. Number of Children
17. Number of People in Household
18. Marital Status
19. Clan or Moeity
20. Caste/Social Class
21. Literate in Which Scripts
22. Religion

It may not be necessary to include every item on this list in every census, but most of them will be quite useful. Just because an item is on the list does not mean it needs to be asked each time an interview is conducted. Information about some items on the list is easily available through inspection. Sex and sometimes occupation fall into this category. Other information is available through deduction. If parents belong to one caste, it is inevitable that their children belong to the same caste. This list is not one which needs to be asked of every individual, rather it is that information which should be known about every individual.

Census information may be conveniently written down in a small, bound notebook, the pages of which have been numbered. Information about one individual goes on one page. If the information on the individual does not come directly from the individual or a member of the individual's household, it should be noted who is giving the information. (13) shows a page from a notebook used for taking census information.

When filling in a census interview sheet, it is better not to leave any blank spots; they are ambiguous. If appropriate, write in a zero or the word 'None'. If the information is unavailable, draw a line through that entry. (13) shows a census sheet which has been filled in for Ramesh, a lifelong inhabitant of Ghaurkhed village. There are nine people residing in his household: himself (Ego); his spouse (Sp); his spouse's mother (SpMo); his eldest son (So1); his son's spouse (So1Sp) and his father (Fa). Each of these people also has a census interview sheet with their biographic information; the number of their interview is cross-referenced with the

Survey on a Shoestring

(13) A Census Interview Sheet

NUMBER OF INTERVIEW: 29
DATE OF INTERVIEW: 860523
LOCATION OF INTERVIEW: Ghaurkhed Village; Kissan County
    Motimahal District

NAME: Ramesh AGE: 35 SEX: M   EDUCATION: 4 OCCUPATION: Farmer
CURRENT RESIDENCE: Ghaurkhed   PREVIOUS OCCUPATION(S): None
PREVIOUS RESIDENCE(S): None   MARITAL STATUS: M
CLAN: None   NUMBER OF CHILDREN: 3
    (only one is over 15)
NUMBER OF PEOPLE IN HOUSEHOLD: 9   MOTHER TONGUE: Pahadi
(1) Sp 30   (2) Ego 29   OTHER TONGUE(S): Hindi (seldom)
(3) SpMo 31   (4) So1 32   Urdu (often)
(5) SoSp 33   (6) Fa 34   LITERATE IN URDU: Yes
(So2, Da3, SoSo are under 15)   LITERATE IN DEVANAGARI: No

appropriate abbreviation. Ramesh's second son (So2), daughter (Da3), and son's son (SoSo) are all under fifteen. Their existence is noted but in this survey no interview sheet was filled out for them. If Ramesh had other relatives living in separate households in the village, the pertinent interview numbers would also be listed here as a means of cross-checking the accuracy of the census.

A village is often a convenient unit from which to gather this sort of information. A village often consists entirely of mother-tongue speakers of the same vernacular and may range in size from a dozen households to several hundred households. A household consists of the people who usually sleep together under a common roof.[5] This information can be gathered in a conversational manner while collecting words for a word list. Each household in the village should be visited. Usually the information about the entire household can be collected from one member of the household. In smaller villages, the census is exhaustive; every household in the community is visited. If the village is a large one, information should be collected on about three to four hundred people, or about one-third of the households belonging to the community, whichever is larger.

It sometimes happens that the community under study does not live in homogeneous villages consisting solely of mother-tongue speakers of the

---

[5]This definition works well in communities where it is the custom for married couples to sleep under the same roof. A different definition may be more useful in places where customs differ.

vernacular. In this case, the goals for the census mentioned above are still valid, but it may not be necessary to visit every household in the village. If mother-tongue speakers of the vernacular are the object of the study, then it is enough to visit only households which use the vernacular as a mother tongue. In this case, however, some effort should be made to determine what percentage of the households in the village are occupied by mother-tongue speakers of the vernacular.

A demographic profile should be developed for more than one village, which means that at least two villages belonging to the same community should have a census conducted in them. The main reason for this is to ensure that the one village in which a census has been completed is not anomalous in some respect. A village which has a school in it may be better educated than a village which does not have a school, which in turn may lead to false assumptions about the level of bilingualism in the total population. A village which is closer to a center of second language use may be more bilingual than a village at a greater distance. In order to ensure the reliability of the data, information should be collected from more than one place.

Conducting a census can be a very time-consuming part of the survey. It is also a fairly intrusive, privacy-disturbing activity. A census should only be attempted in a village in which at least one of the researchers is well known, in order to avoid suspicion, hostility, and the chance of collecting false data. Given good contacts, it takes about two weeks to gather the information listed above concerning the requisite number of people. In spite of the fact that it is time-consuming and sometimes difficult, it is necessary information for the accurate planning and interpretation of a survey. In some cases, it may be possible to gain access to existing government census data. This information can be quite useful and helpful. Nevertheless, caution must be exercised in the use of such data. In some cases it is not accurate; in other cases it was gathered for reasons other than a bilingualism study. In the latter case, the different presuppositions with which the census was done may render it invalid for use in a bilingualism project.

Number, date, and location of interview. Even if information concerning several people comes from the same person, it may be recorded as though these were separate interviews. Put all the information concerning one person on the same census interview sheet. If desired, a notation can be made as to the identity of the person being interviewed, if it is different from the person with whom the data are concerned. If the surveyor is using a small notebook to record census information, then the pages should be numbered. The page number then suffices as the interview number also. Most interviews are conducted in the same place as the current residence, but if not, it is sometimes useful to know who was interviewed where. It is a good practice to record the date the information was collected for future reference.

Name. Record enough of a person's name to distinguish the individual from other individuals. In some communities it is not appropriate for individuals to give their own personal names, but it is usually possible to elicit some sort of identifying name or nickname. In places where a single name is all that is commonly used, it may be helpful to record the name of one of the individual's parents. Keeping track of the name of a spouse would serve much the same purpose, but in some communities it is often not acceptable practice for an individual to give the spouse's name.

Age. In many communities, age may be a difficult item of information to elicit accurately. Birth certificates and medical records may be uncommon. Even assuming that individuals do know their age, people in many of the world's cultures feel no compulsion to accurately state their age for a stranger. Determining age on the basis of physical appearance is also fraught with difficulties.

Often the most that can be done is to fit people into one of four broad generational categories: children (1–15), youths (16–30), adults (31–45), and elders (46 and over). Children who do not yet show the secondary sex characteristics associated with the onset of puberty are usually under sixteen years of age. If an individual's oldest child has reached puberty, then that individual is likely to be over thirty. If an individual's oldest grandchild has reached puberty, then that individual is likely to be over 45 years of age. (The converse of these two statements is not necessarily true, of course.) Individuals who have reached puberty, but have never yet been married are generally under thirty years of age. Children's ages are more frequently known than those of adults, and knowing the age of the oldest child is frequently helpful in determining the age of parents. It may also be helpful to know at what age men and women are expected to marry in the community in question, as well as what the difference in age between a man and his wife is expected to be. It is also useful to know the order in which siblings were born. If the youngest of a set of siblings has just reached puberty, it is often possible to accurately place the older siblings to within five years of their age, especially if the age difference between siblings is known.

Sex. Normally, this is a two-valued characteristic which can easily be determined by inspection.

Education. Normally, this characteristic is best thought of in terms of number of years of formal schooling. This often coincides with the number of 'grades' or 'standards' of school which an individual has attended. It is a good idea for the researcher to be familiar with the educational system extant in the community that is being studied. In many parts of South Asia, the school culminates at tenth standard with an exam for a School-Leaving Certificate (SLC). Students who have taken this exam are referred to either as 'SLC-pass' or 'SLC-fail', depending on their marks on the exam. Both terms usually imply ten years of schooling. A student who has an 'SLC-pass' may then proceed directly to the university (in exceptional cases) or, more commonly, take one or two years of preuniversity training. A student who has finished two years of such training is said to have 'ten plus two', while a student with only one year is 'ten plus one'. Following preuniversity training, there are various undergraduate degrees, with various requirements in terms of number of years required. It is not uncommon for people to refer to themselves as 'B.A. pass' or 'B.A. fail'. The latter indicates that the student attended the courses, but was unable to pass the requisite exams. The number of years required to complete graduate and undergraduate degrees differs widely from individual to individual. All of this indicates that eliciting useful information about education attainments is not as simple as asking "How much school have you had?" In some cases even an apparently simple answer like "First grade" may mean that the individual never got further than first grade, though he attended it for three years in a row.

In some communities, the language of education will be different for different members of the community. In these cases it is useful to record which language was the medium of instruction for a particular individual.

Occupation. OCCUPATION is a category which is more important in communities which practice a division or specialization of labor among their members. In communities in which everyone has nearly the same skills, and does nearly the same thing for a living, this category has little meaning. In some cases it can be used to designate sociopolitical roles in the community, with 'occupations' such as village head, village council member, village healer, etc. In other cases, particularly in some agricultural communities, it can be used to distinguish those who own and farm their own land from those who hire out their agricultural services for a daily wage.

In some communities which practice labor specialization, it is not uncommon for people to have had occupations different from the ones they hold at the time of the interview. It is important to inquire about past occupations for some of them might have brought the individual into substantially more contact with speakers of a second language than is usually the case for members of that community. For example, an older man who is now a farmer may be substantially more bilingual than his neighbors because he is the only member of the community to have served in the military. A woman may be substantially more bilingual than her neighbors because she worked as day labor on a nearby coffee plantation before she was married.

Place of residence. A census should always record the PLACE OF CURRENT RESIDENCE in order to ensure that the person being interviewed is actually a member of the village in which the census is being carried out. Most villages have a temporary population of visiting friends and relatives, who are staying in the village for greater or shorter lengths of time, but who are generally recognized to belong to a different place. It is generally best not to include such people in the census information for that particular village.

Even the most stable of villages usually have people currently living there who were not born there. It is often the case that some of the people in the village have brought their spouses from other places. It is sometimes the case that someone from another village has either bought or inherited land in the village being studied, and so has moved there. When carrying out a census it is necessary to inquire about previous places of residence in order to account for some variations in bilingual ability. For example, if a large number of the men of a village marry women from a village that is closer to a center of second language use, it may be that some of the women of the village are more bilingual than others on the basis of previous residence.

Religion. Many communities are homogeneous with regard to RELIGION. This category is probably unnecessary in such cases. In other communities religious beliefs can be quite diverse and may influence bilingual ability. For example, in many parts of South Asia, Muslims are more likely to be bilingual in Urdu than non-Muslims of the same ethnolinguistic community.

Social class. Some linguistic communities are relatively homogeneous with regard to social subdivisions, others are not. The importance of recording the particular subdivision to which an individual belongs depends upon the community. In some communities it will not be necessary. In others it may be necessary to record more than one social subdivision. For example, if a linguistic community consists of several different castes and each caste consisted of several clans, it might be the case that various castes, and various clans in each caste have more dealings with speakers of the second language than other clans.

Household. Marital status, number of children, and number of people in household are three categories included in order to help check the thoroughness of the information gathered. If it is known how many people live in the house being visited, it is easy to determine when the census for the people in that household has been completed. On the page of the notebook that has the information for the oldest person in the household, list the interview numbers of all the other people living in that household and their relationship to the oldest person. The abbreviations in (14) are useful in summarizing relationships.

(14) 1. Spouse   Sp   5. Sister   Si
      2. Son   So   6. Father   Fa
      3. Daughter   Da   7. Mother   Mo
      4. Brother   Br

If there is, or has been, more than one spouse, the oldest can be designated with a (1) and the next with a (2). With these seven basic abbreviations, combinations like those in (15) are possible.

(15) Son's Son   SoSo
      Son's Daughter   SoDa
      Daughter's Son   DaSo
      Daughter's Daughter   DaDa
      Brother's Spouse   BrSp
      Spouse's Brother   SpBr
      Brother's Son   BrSo
      Sister's Spouse   SiSp
      Spouse's Sister   SpSi
      Sister's Son's Spouse SiSoSp

Such measures to keep track of the number of people in a household are useful in communities where it is common for joint or extended families to live together under the same roof.

Keeping track of the number of children is also useful in checking on the thoroughness of a census. Record this information for each mother. If the mother is no longer in the household, but the children still are, then record the number of children with the father. It is usually not necessary to record much information about children younger than fifteen, other than the fact that they exist. In some studies it might be useful to keep track of which children are going to school and how many years they have attended.

Marital Status is usually one of four possibilities—Married (M), Widow/Widower (W), Divorced/Separated (D), and Unmarried (S). Since most societies practice either serial or concurrent polygamy, several of these states may be true for one person. If a man has more than one wife living with him in the household, record the children (under fifteen years of age) of each wife with their mother. If the mother of children living in the household is no longer present, record them with their father or other relative. If a woman has more than one husband, record all of her children with her. Grown children (over fifteen years of age) generally have a page devoted to them.

First language. An individual's MOTHER TONGUE is that person's first language, the language that was spoken with the parents as a child. In many cases it is the language most frequently used with other family members. Difficulties in ascertaining the mother tongue sometimes arise in communities undergoing language shift. Sometimes children speak one language with their father and another with their mother. Such cases should be noted.

Second languages. When recording what other languages an individual uses, it is helpful to get a rough self-estimate of the individual's ability in or frequency of use of that language. This can be done by asking if the person uses the language rarely (less than once a month), seldom (several times a month), often (several times a week), or frequently (several times a day). For example, a person who goes to the market every week may use the second language there and no place else. The market is the major domain of the second language. Since it is possible to determine how frequently the individual goes to the market, it is not difficult to determine the frequency of use in this domain. In this the frequency could be rated as SELDOM. Or parents may use the second language every day when they speak to their children; in this case frequency of second language use could be rated as FREQUENT.

Scripts. In some communities several SCRIPTS are in use for different languages. It is important to record which scripts (if any) the individual is able to read and write.

Analysis of census data. When the census data have been collected, it is necessary to analyze them. Census data collected according to the instructions contained in the previous section contain information on a variety of social characteristics that influence bilingualism. They also include some sort of self-reported data on bilingual ability. The self-reported data on bilingual ability may not be very reliable, but they provide a place to start examining those characteristics which are of particular interest in affecting bilingualism in the community.

Tabulation. When census interviews have been completed, the data consist of two or three hundred pages of information. Each page contains all the information gathered about one individual. Although this effectively organizes the information, it is difficult to make generalizations directly from data arranged in this fashion. In order to use data more effectively they must be tabulated.

TABULATION is the process of counting how frequently various social characteristics, and combinations of characteristics, occur in the data. It is a simple, though tedious, process. The first step is to identify the various categories, or values, that occur for each social characteristic. For example, sex has two possible values—male and female. Education, on the other hand, has several possible values, depending on how it is measured. A common measurement, the number of years of education, has a number of possible values—zero, one, two, three, etc. Which of these values occur is different in each community. A social characteristic like clan, may not exist at all in some communities, and thus there will be no value for it.

The second step in tabulating the data is to identify the FREQUENCY with which the various values of each social characteristic occur. For example, the number of men and the number of women must be counted. In many communities, the number of men should approximately equal the number of women, give or take five percent.[6] This fact provides a way of checking the integrity of the data that have been collected. If the data do show men and women to be present in about equal numbers, this does not ensure that the data are accurate in other respects, but if the data do not show such equality, there may be a problem with the way they were collected.

Age data can also be checked for integrity. Some of the problems with collecting age data have already been discussed. There is a tendency to round off uncertain figures for age to the nearest five or ten. The data can be checked to see if ages ending with five or zero occur more frequently than they ought. It has already been mentioned that it is frequently more useful to deal with age in terms of fifteen year spans, rather than with

---

[6]There are exceptions to this rule of thumb. Some communities are seminomadic, or are dependent upon migrant labor, both of which often mean that one sex or the other is underrepresented. In other communities, environmental or cultural factors may be more hostile to one or the other of the sexes, again resulting in underrepresentation.

Survey on a Shoestring

precise individual ages. If this is the case, then 'age' generally has four values rather than sixty or so. See the discussion of age in the previous section.

A third step in tabulating the data is done after the census has been analyzed and the independent variables and values for those variables relevant to the study have been identified. This consists of tabulating the frequency of various combinations of values for the social characteristics. In the second step of tabulation, it is enough to know how many men and how many women there are; how many people with one year of education, and how many with two years, etc. This information is needed to decide on the variables and their values to be included in the sample. In the third step of tabulation, it is necessary to know what percentage of the population consists of middle-aged males with a primary school education. In this case, three independent variables have been included in the samples—age, sex, and education. Values for those variables have also been decided upon and defined. 'Male' and 'female' are the values for sex. Middle-aged is one of the values for age, and primary school education is one of the values for the education variable.

Functions of analysis. Analysis of census data has three functions in studies of bilingualism and language use and attitude in a community. The first is DIAGNOSTIC. Analysis identifies the independent variables which must be included in the sample. For example, education often correlates with an increase in bilingual ability. In any study, therefore, the question arises as to whether or not educated people should be included in the sample. Analysis of census data will determine whether education is common enough that education is likely to be an important variable. If more than ten percent of the population has some education, then it is likely that educated people should be included in the sample. As a rule of thumb, if any of the social characteristics mentioned in the previous section describe ten percent or more of the population of the community under study, and bilingual ability as reported by individuals appears to change according to value of the characteristic, then it is probably important to include that characteristic in the sample. (This does not mean that characteristics less common than ten percent would necessarily be excluded. Sometimes a small portion of the population is an important one.) As a practical matter, this means that age and sex are two social characteristics which almost always must be included in any sample as independent variables.

The second function of census data analysis is to DETERMINE THE VALUES OF THE INDEPENDENT VARIABLES that will be included in the sample. For some independent variables the values are obvious. For example, sex has two possible values. For other independent variables, the relevant values are not so obvious. For example, if education is one of the independent variables that must be included in the sample, should it have two values (no education and some education) or should it have three values (no education, a primary school education, and secondary school education)? Or perhaps the number of years spent in school is the relevant value for the variable. Analysis of census data helps to determine the categories (values) under which test subjects are grouped. If a third of the population has had no education, a third has had part of a primary school education, and the final third has had part of a secondary school education, then those values would be reasonable subdivisions for the sample.

The third function of census data analysis is INTERPRETIVE. When data collection is complete and it comes time to draw conclusions about the extent of bilingualism in a population, it is the census data which determine what the survey results mean in terms of people. For example, survey results may show that educated women are the most bilingual segment of the population. It is the analysis of census data which says that educated women make up 25 percent of the population.

4.3 Summary

This section has discussed determining sample composition as an important preliminary to sociolinguistic research, with a special emphasis on its role in evaluating bilingualism. A sample should be adequately representative of the population from which it is drawn. In order to do this the social characteristics which are likely to influence the dependent variable being studied need to be understood, and their existence and distribution in the community must be ascertained.

A demographic profile of the community identifies the frequency and distribution in the community of the various social characteristics under consideration. The information in a demographic profile is derived from systematic information about the community gathered with a census questionnaire. Special problems in gathering the various kinds of information in the census have been discussed.

5
Bilingualism

> Since our concern was speech, and speech impelled us
> To purify the language of the tribe.
>
> T. S. Eliot
> *Little Gidding*

5.1 Introduction

The goal of a study of community bilingualism is to find out how bilingual the population of a community is. Bilingualism is not a characteristic which is uniformly distributed. In any community, different individuals or sections of the community are bilingual to different degrees. It is important to avoid characterizing an entire community as though such ability were uniformly distributed. It is more accurate to describe how bilingualism is distributed throughout the community.

There are various ways of identifying the bilingual competence of different people. These may be referred to as bilingualism evaluation methods. Most bilingual evaluation methods depend on the factors in which particular researchers are most interested. One of the best known methods for assigning individuals to a particular level of bilingualism is that developed by the Foreign Service Institute (FSI) of the U.S. Department of State. An adaption of this appears in Brewster and Brewster (1976:374–76). There are, however, other ways of assigning an individual to a particular level of bilingual ability which do not depend either on the FSI levels or oral proficiency interviewing. The various methods of evaluating bilingual ability are discussed in subsequent chapters. This chapter is concerned with the ways in which bilingual ability may be distributed among the different sections of a community.

There are two parts to a study of bilingual ability in a community. Assigning an individual to a level of bilingual ability is only one part. Though bilingual ability is usually not uniformly distributed throughout a community, there is a patterned distribution of bilingual ability in many communities. People at similar levels of bilingual ability often have another social characteristic in common which accounts for their having similar bilingual abilities. This chapter discusses the various social characteristics which often influence bilingualism and how these different factors correlate. In a study of community bilingualism, the level of bilingualism of an individual is treated as the dependent variable and the various social characteristics which influence bilingualism (e.g., education, age, sex, degree of contact with speakers of the second language, etc.) are treated as the independent variables. Two hypotheses are possible: (a) There is a correlation between bilingualism and one of the independent variables (or a cluster of independent variables) or (b) There is no correlation between bilingualism and one of the independent variables identified in the study (this is sometimes called the 'null hypothesis'.)

Once a correlation has been established between degree of bilingualism and an independent variable, it remains to be seen how that particular independent variable is distributed throughout the community. If there is a high degree of correlation between age and bilingualism, then the older someone is, the more likely that individual is to be bilingual. It then becomes important to know what portion of the population is at different ages so that it is possible to tell what portions of a community are likely to be at what levels of bilingual ability. If people over 45 years of age are likely to be at the highest level of bilingualism, and 20 percent of the population is over 45 years of age, then at least 20 percent of the population is likely to be at the highest level of bilingualism. (This is, of course, a very simple example.) Chapter 4 contains a discussion of how to discover the distribution of various social characteristics throughout a population.

Bilingualism refers to the knowledge and skills acquired by individuals which enable them to use a language other than their mother tongue. Bilingualism may be characteristic of communities as well as individuals, for bilingual individuals rarely exist apart from a bilingual community. Most often individuals are bilingual precisely because of community needs and pressures.

An individual or a community becomes bilingual when both motivation and opportunity exist. When it is in an individual's or a community's self-perceived best interest to become bilingual, motivation toward bilingualism exists. The motivation may be economic or religious; it may be self-preservation or it may be altruistic. The community will become as

Survey on a Shoestring

bilingual as it deems necessary in order to satisfy its self-interest. The extent of the motivation will determine to a large extent how much of the second language they desire to learn.

The level of bilingualism attained by an individual or a community depends not only upon motivation but also upon opportunities to acquire the second language. People cannot become bilingual unless they have contact with the second language in some context. The degree of contact they have with speakers of the second language will determine to a large extent how much of the second language they are able to learn.

Motivation and contact are the two most important factors which produce bilingualism. In studies of the distribution of bilingual ability throughout a community, the level of bilingualism is the dependent variable, while motivation and opportunity (as represented by degree of contact) are independent variables. Both factors must be present for bilingualism to occur. (16) portrays the relationship between these variables.

(16) Contact
                    ⟶ Bilingualism
       Motivation

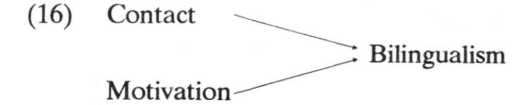

Degree of contact and motivation are difficult to measure as variables; the factors which influence them are easier to quantify. Insights into a community's motivation to learn a second language can often be gained by identifying the domains in which the second language is used. This is discussed in the section on language use and attitude studies. The degree of contact with the second language may correlate directly with such variables as education, occupation, military service, age, sex, frequency of contact with mother-tongue speakers of the second language, etc. (17) illustrates the relationship between these factors.

(17) Education
      Occupation
      Age   ⟶ Contact
      Sex   ⟶ Bilingualism
      Other   Motivation

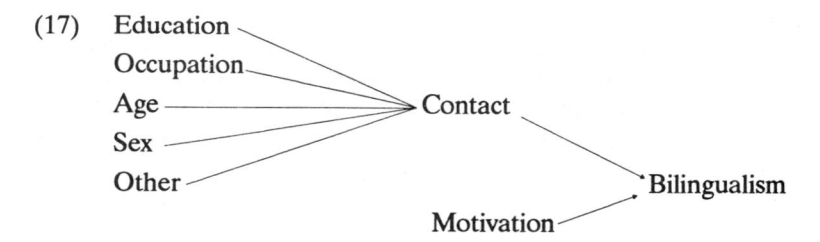

As (17) shows, the relationship between various social characteristics and bilingualism is not direct. These various social characteristics combine in different ways to determine how much contact an individual is likely to have with the second language. According to this model, only two variables have direct influence increasing the level of bilingualism. For most purposes, however, we shall treat the various social characteristics mentioned here as the independent variables, in place of degree of contact.

5.2 Social Characteristics Influencing Bilingualism

The following discussion of the social characteristics which influence bilingualism treats each of the variables as though it were a discrete unit. In fact, this is rarely the case. More often a constellation of factors are acting together in determining the degree of contact an individual or community has with other speakers of the second language. A study of community bilingualism attempts to correlate various social characteristics with the levels of bilingualism of individuals in that community. This section looks at social characteristics such as age, sex, education, etc. and discusses how they tend to correlate with bilingualism. A study of community bilingualism must also assess the frequency with which these characteristics occur in the whole community. The section on demographic profiles discusses ways to do this. Assuming that the relevant social characteristics have been identified and that a correlation between a particular level of bilingualism and those characteristics exists, it should be possible to derive an accurate picture of the bilingual ability of the community from these two kinds of information. There are, therefore, two steps to any study of community bilingualism. The first is to identify the independent variables, those social characteristics which correlate with bilingualism, and their distribution throughout the community. The second is assessing the dependent variable, the level of bilingualism which occurs in conjunction with the various characteristics.

Age. The age of an individual is one variable which commonly influences how bilingual that person is. Bilingualism and age may interact in at least three ways. Bilingualism may decrease with age; bilingualism may increase with age; or bilingual ability may peak about middle age. These are not the only possible situations, but they are the more common ones. In any community in which bilingualism appears to correlate with youth, it is sometimes the case that a stronger correlation with another variable, such as level of education,[7] will account for it. For the sake of simplicity, this

---

[7]In this discussion I have assumed that the medium of instruction is the second language, as is commonly the case. Should the medium of instruction be the vernacular or a third language these give rise to somewhat different situations. These are discussed in the section on education.

Survey on a Shoestring

discussion looks at age independent of most of the other variables which may also be influencing bilingualism.

In some communities younger people are the more bilingual segment of the population. (18) illustrates this situation.

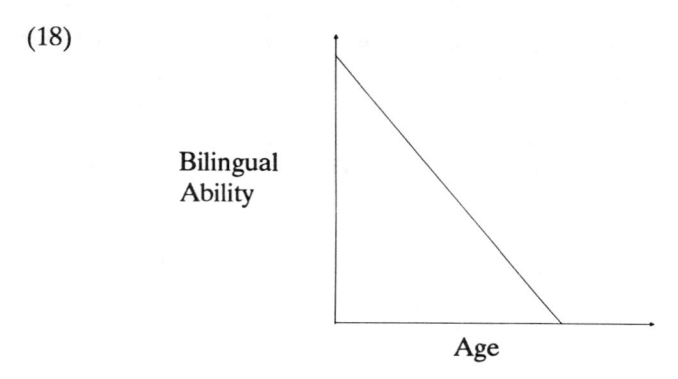

(18)

```
    Bilingual
    Ability
                    Age
```

This is often true in communities where members of the younger generation tend to be better educated than members of the older generation. In cases like this, education is often the important variable; it just happens that education in some communities correlates strongly with youth. In a few communities it is the case that the older generation is better educated; in communities like these, a higher level of bilingualism correlates with increasing age.

In many communities older people are more bilingual, not necessarily because they are better educated, in the formal sense of having gone to school longer, but because they have lived longer and so had more opportunity to learn the second language. (19) illustrates this situation.

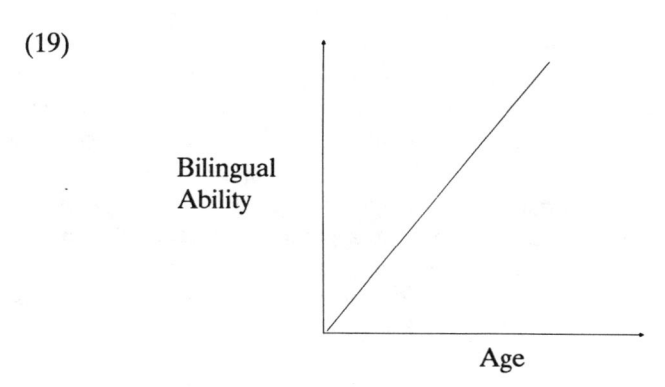

(19)

```
    Bilingual
    Ability
                    Age
```

In some communities, it is the role of the older people to make any arrangements with outsiders that need to be made. This also contributes to a greater degree of bilingualism among older people than among younger. In communities where formal education has not yet penetrated, children and youths are often the least bilingual segment of the population. In such communities, however, it does not necessarily follow that the oldest people will be the most bilingual.

In some communities bilingual ability will peak with middle age and decline thereafter, depending on the roles various age groups have in dealing with people who speak the second language. (20) illustrates this situation.

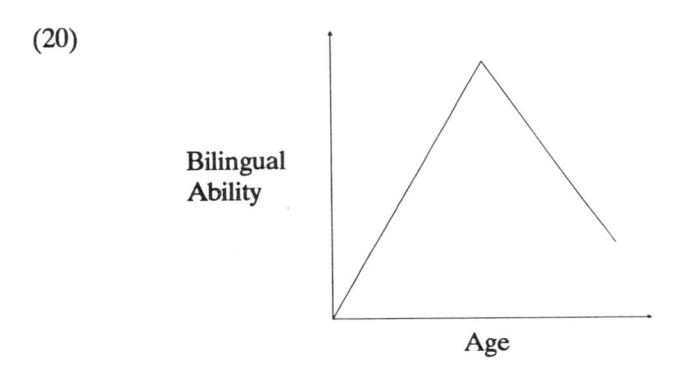

(20)

[Graph: Bilingual Ability (y-axis) vs. Age (x-axis), showing a triangular peak curve]

There are many possible reasons for this decline; these differ from community to community. In some cases it is because middle aged people are the ones who have the most to do with outsiders. Bilingual ability may decrease over time if it is not practiced. Older people who are no longer as active as they once were in dealing with outsiders may begin to lose the bilingual ability they once had.

Another factor which sometimes causes a high level of bilingualism to correlate with middle age is education. It sometimes happens that a newly initiated educational system functions well for the first twenty years of its life. This gives rise to a situation like that where bilingual ability decreases with age. If something happens to disrupt the educational system for a period of time, the younger people lose an opportunity to learn the second language that their parents were able to acquire. Because the educational system was initiated when the current oldest generation was already past school age, they also may not be very bilingual.

Sex. The sex of individuals is another variable which commonly influences their bilingual ability. The distribution of bilingual ability between the sexes is often a function of their respective social roles in the community. Here also there are three possible situations. Women may be more bilingual than men; men may be more bilingual than women; or the bilingual ability of the sexes may be about the same. As is the case with age, any correlation between bilingual ability and sex should be checked to ensure that the data do not show a stronger correlation with another variable, such as education. For the sake of simplicity, we will treat sex as though it operated independently of most other variables which may also be influencing bilingualism.

In some communities women may be among the more bilingual segments of the community. This may occur for a variety of reasons. In some communities women may have more education than men. If the second language is the medium of instruction, it then follows that women would have more opportunity to acquire the second language. In other communities, it may be that the women are the ones who have more to do with outsiders. For example, if the women of the community are the ones who do most of the buying and selling, they may have more contact with people who speak the second language than the men of the community. In communities where it is not uncommon for the men to marry women who belong to a community which uses the second language as its mother tongue, it is not unusual to find that women have a much higher level of ability in that language than the men do.

The reasons for men being more bilingual than women in some communities are similar to those discussed for women. In some communities men have better access to education in the second language than do women. In other communities, men are the ones who do most of the buying and selling and so are the ones who normally deal with outsiders. In some very conservative communities, women rarely have an opportunity to speak with anyone who does not control the vernacular and so never have an opportunity to acquire the second language.

In many communities there is no difference in the bilingual ability of men and of women. In communities which have little or no contact with speakers of the second language, it is unlikely that either sex will have the opportunity to acquire much knowledge of a second language. In communities where both men and women have about the same access to education, it is likely that both sexes will be roughly equal with regard to bilingual ability. Communities which make few distinctions in social roles on the basis of sex are likely to have both sexes functioning at about the same levels of bilingual ability.

Education. Education and bilingualism is a complex topic compared to those mentioned previously. Much depends on which language is used for education and on its place in the overall linguistic environment in the region. I discuss three situations here. The most common situation in the types of communities where we have been doing survey is where the second language is both the regional language of wider communication and the language of education. Another common situation is when the second language serves only as the regional language of wider communication and a third language serves as the language of education. A third situation occurs when the second language is the regional language of wider communication while the vernacular is used as the language of education. As has been mentioned previously, it is only rarely that one variable alone can account for the level of bilingual ability present in a population. Nevertheless, for simplicity's sake the following discussion treats education as an isolated factor.

When the second language is both the regional language of wider communication and the language of education, bilingual ability will increase with the level of education. If a community has little or no contact with speakers of the second language, bilingual ability starts at near zero and remains there for the first few of years of education. (21) illustrates this situation.

(21) Bilingual Ability Increases with Education: Little Contact with Second-language Speakers

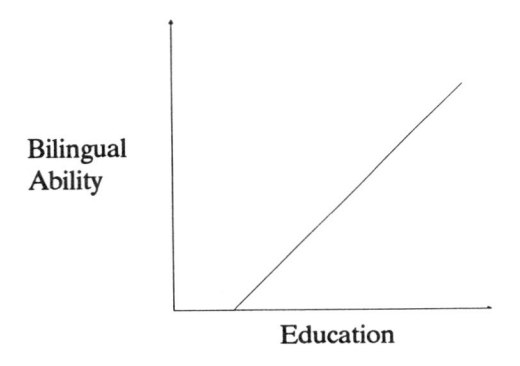

In a community which has limited contact with speakers of the second language, there is little chance for people to use what knowledge of the second language they have acquired in school. Without such reinforcement, bilingual ability is likely to remain near zero among that portion of the population with only a few years of school. Those who continue on in school depend on their knowledge of the second language for whatever academic success they are capable of, and so their bilingual ability increases steadily with further education.

Survey on a Shoestring

If a community has a high degree of contact with speakers of the second language, bilingual ability may be present regardless of level of education. People who have had one or two years of schooling may be just as bilingual as people who have had five or six years. (22) illustrates this situation.

(22) Bilingual Ability Increases with Education: High Degree of Contact with Second-language Speakers

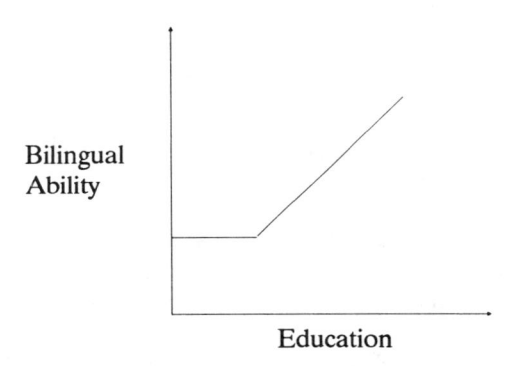

In a community that has a lot of contact with speakers of the second language, most people have an opportunity to acquire some knowledge of the second language. Therefore everyone is likely to have some basic competence in the second language. However, those who continue longer in school than is typical for the community will steadily acquire more and more of the second language.

In some communities two languages beside the vernacular are used for different purposes. One of these fulfills the role of a language of wider communication and serves the purpose of communicating with other people in the same region who do not control that community's vernacular. Another language is the medium of instruction in the schools. In a situation like this, it is often necessary to assess bilingual ability in both languages. (23) illustrates this situation.

As (23) shows, bilingual ability in the second language, the language of wider communication, remains relatively constant regardless of level of education. Bilingual ability in the third language, the language of education, increases steadily with level of education.

An unusual situation occurs in communities where a second language has traditionally been the language of education, but political changes in the recent past have caused this second language to be displaced by a third in the domain of education. This situation is not infrequent in areas where political

(23) Bilingual Ability in Two Languages: the Second Language is the Regional Language; the Third Language is the Language of Education

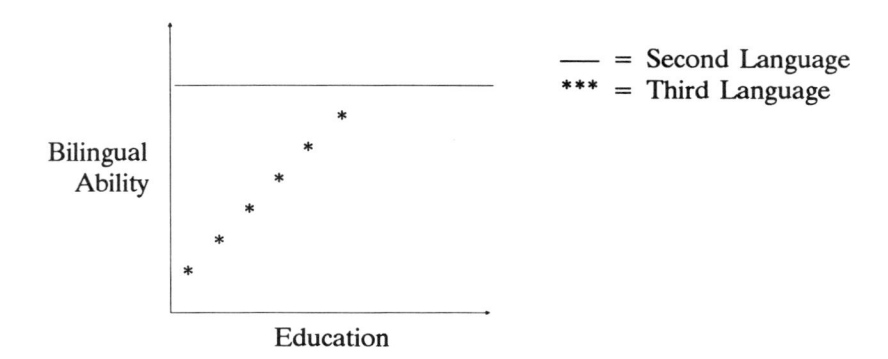

```
                                            ——— = Second Language
              |  _____         ***  = Third Language
              |
              |              *
  Bilingual   |          *
   Ability    |        *
              |      *
              |    *
              |  *
              |_____
                    Education
```

boundaries have recently changed. In some communities the change in the language used for education is a sign that an overall language shift is underway; in other communities, the change has been limited only to the educational domain.

If bilingual ability in each of the two languages is correlated with age, older people who have been educated in the second language will often have less bilingual ability in the third language. When the language used in education has changed to a third language, younger people will be more bilingual in the third language than older people, while older people may be more bilingual than younger people in the second language. (24) shows this situation.

(24) Bilingual Ability in Two Languages: The Medium of Instruction Changed a Generation Ago

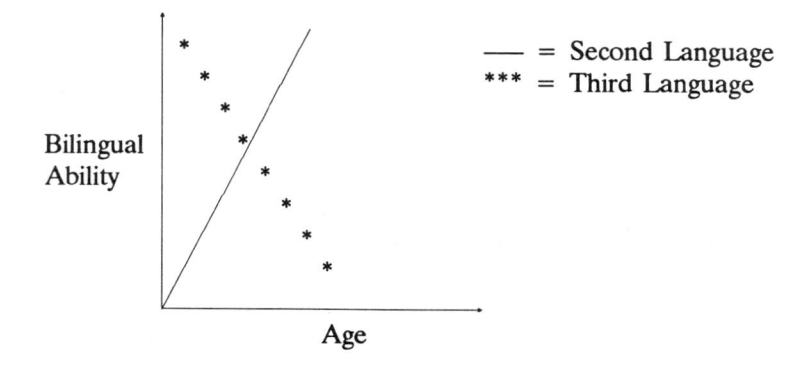

```
              |  *         /
              |    *      /               ——— = Second Language
              |      *   /                ***  = Third Language
  Bilingual   |        */
   Ability    |        / *
              |       /    *
              |      /       *
              |     /          *
              |____/_____
                      Age
```

Survey on a Shoestring 61

A variation on this situation occurs when education itself is a fairly recent introduction to the community. In some communities, education in the regional language of wider communication was the first formal education to become available. More recently, however, the language of education was shifted to a third language not as widely spoken in the area. If a survey is carried out at a time when most of the older people are those who never had a chance to go to school, then the correlation of bilingual ability in the second language will show a peak among the middle-aged people in the community, as (25) shows.

(25) Bilingual Ability in Two Languages: Education Introduced Recently in the Second Language and Changed to the Third Language

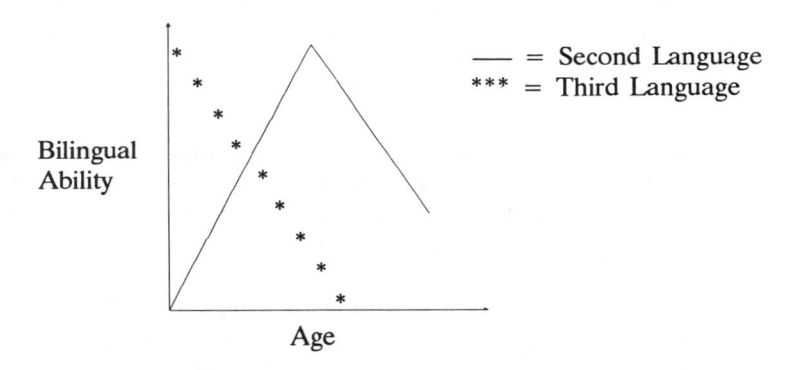

```
                          ——— = Second Language
                          *** = Third Language
```

Bilingual Ability

Age

In (25), bilingual ability in both the second and third language decreases among the oldest people because education in the either language is an opportunity that was not available to these people.

Language shift in the education domain from a regional language of wider communication to a third language is not the only direction language shift may go. In some communities the opposite shift has occurred. When a third language which is only used in the education domain is given up even in that domain in favor of a widely spoken regional language of wider communication, a community's bilingual ability in the third language often decreases rapidly.

When the vernacular is the language of education, there is often no correlation between level of education and bilingual ability in the second language unless the second language is also being taught in the school. If the second language is being taught in the school as well as the vernacular, there may be a correlation between education and ability in the second language.

The language of education in some communities may have been the second language in the recent past, but the language of education is now the vernacular. If this is the case, then it may be that education and ability in the second language will correlate among those educated before the shift was made, but there will probably be no correlation between education and second language ability among those who have been educated since the shift was made (unless the second language is also taught as a subject in the school).

The opposite shift may have occurred in some communities in the recent past. The language of education may then have been the vernacular, but it is now the second language. If this is the case, it may be that education and ability in the second language will correlate among those educated after the shift was made, but there will probably be no correlation between education and second language ability among those who were educated before the shift was made. An exception would be if the second language is also taught as a subject in the school during the time when the vernacular was the medium of instruction.

Frequency of Contact. As mentioned, the acquisition of bilingualism by a community or an individual depends on two things: motivation and contact. Age, sex, and education are social characteristics which often correlate strongly with opportunity for contact with speakers of the second language. The correlation may be direct or indirect, depending on the community. Because the ways in which these variables correlate with bilingualism is complex and often depends on conditions peculiar to the community in which bilingualism is being studied, they have been discussed separately and at length in the foregoing sections. Several other variables (e.g., travel, occupation, proximity to center of second language use, etc.) also often correlate with frequency of contact. It is the nature of the social characteristics discussed in this section to provide opportunity for greater frequency of contact with speakers of the second language. As bilingual ability is generally greater among those portions of the community which have more contact, each of these social characteristics generally correlates with greater bilingual ability, as (26) shows.

Travel. Frequent and consistent travels to places where an individual's vernacular is not spoken often correlates strongly with a high degree of bilingual ability in an individual. Business trips, tourism, job hunting, and visiting family relations sometimes point to this factor being an important one in the case of some individuals. It sometimes is the case that a few highly bilingual individuals in a community that is otherwise not very bilingual have spent several years of their lives in an area where knowledge

(26) Bilingual Ability Increases with Frequency of Contact with Speakers of the Second Language

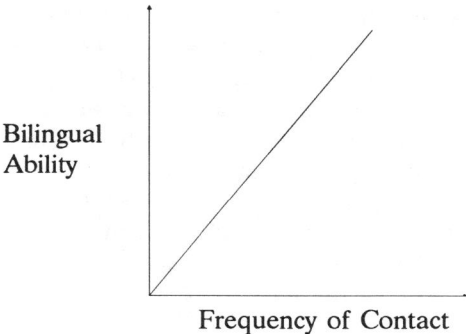

[Graph: Bilingual Ability (y-axis) vs. Frequency of Contact (x-axis), showing a linear increasing relationship.]

of the second language is necessary. For this reason, it is not enough to inquire only after frequency and consistency of travel to places outside of the area in which the vernacular is used. It is also necessary to find out if individuals have spent part of their life outside of the area in which the vernacular is used. Education (e.g., boarding school), occupation (e.g., seminomadic herdsmen), or family relations (e.g., exogamous marriage relationships) are all reasons which sometimes cause individuals to spend significant portions of their lives in places where acquisition of a second language is necessary.

Individual travel is not the only sort of travel likely to correlate with bilingualism. Either an entire community or a portion of a community may be nomadic. Nomadic portions of a community may differ markedly from non-nomadic portions in bilingual ability, depending on how much contact with speakers of the second language the two portions have. Mendicant and pastoral nomadic groups often make an attempt to adopt whatever language is most widely spoken in the areas through which they travel. This language is mostly used for communicating with people who are not members of their group. Mercantile nomadic groups sometimes make an attempt to learn the various languages of the different people groups they have to deal with, presumably in order to bargain more effectively. Nomadic groups of all sorts often retain the vernacular for communication within the group; the fact that no one from outside the group is able to understand the vernacular may be a valued asset. Bilingual ability within a nomadic group may vary depending on the degree of contact different members have with outsiders.

Occupation. Occupation is another variable which may correlate with bilingualism. Certain occupations often require a knowledge of the regional language of wider communication as a condition of employment. Other occupations bring individuals into a greater degree of contact with speakers of the second language than is commonly the case for members of the community in general. Still others, particularly professional occupations, entail the acquisition of a second language as part of the training for the occupation. Similarly, in many communities, bilingual ability is often a prerequisite for anyone who wishes to hold a position of leadership.

Current occupation is not the only way in which occupation may affect bilingual ability. It is necessary in some cases to check for past occupations in order to account for anomalies in a study of bilingualism. In particular past military service sometimes correlates with an unusual degree of bilingual ability.

Religion. In some communities religious variety correlates with bilingual ability in various languages. In some cases this bilingual ability is strictly limited to the religious domain; in other cases the use of a particular second language is characteristic of a religious identification.

Proximity. If frequency of contact is a factor which correlates directly with bilingual ability, it should not be surprising that proximity to speakers of the second language has an effect on frequency of contact. Geographical proximity is not the critical factor, for in many multilingual areas travel time and geographical proximity are quite different matters. But in many communities, those people who dwell closer, either geographically or temporally, to speakers of the second language are more bilingual.

In some communities, having a next door neighbor who is a speaker of the second language is enough to ensure a greater degree of bilingualism. Other communities tend to be settled in monolingual clusters. In these communities, those clusters closer to the road, the market, or another settlement where the second language is used may be more bilingual than those who live farther away.

5.3 Bilingualism evaluation methods

> That Heresies should arise, we have the prophesie of Christ; but that old ones should be abolished, we hold no prediction.
>
> Thomas Browne, 1642
> *Religio Medici,I,8*

There are several ways of evaluating bilingual ability. This is because there is no general agreement on exactly what bilingual ability is. Each method of evaluating bilingual ability tests something different from the other methods discussed in this section. Some of the methods focus on comprehension of the second language. Others focus on the ability to speak in the second language. Still others try to balance both the comprehension and production aspects of bilingual ability. Different tests are useful for different purposes in a survey. It is recommended that a study of bilingualism use more than one method of evaluating bilingual ability.

Tests are administered to the individuals who compose the sample. Each of the tests yields a score. These scores are often referred to as the level of bilingual ability. A higher score is assumed to correspond with a higher level of bilingual ability. It is difficult to compare a score given by one test with a score from another test because most of the tests are measuring different things. For example, a score on a recorded text test is usually expressed as a percentage of questions answered correctly. A score on a sentence repetition test is a subset of the total points awarded for the accuracy with which a set of sentences was repeated. A score on an oral proficiency test reflects the judgment of an evaluator as to where the bilingual ability of an individual being tested lies on a scale from zero to five. As yet no strong correlation between a score on one test and a score on another test has been established. A variety of opinions exist on this subject and these are discussed in the sections which deal with each test.

5.4 Summary

This section has examined some of the ways in which bilingualism may be distributed in a community. Bilingual ability is understood to be a characteristic of both individuals and communities. People become bilingual in accordance with their motivation and the amount of contact they have with speakers of the second language. Various social characteristics which often correlate with amount of contact—such as age, sex, education, and frequency of contact—were discussed. Bilingualism evaluation methods must be used in a way which discovers the pattern of distribution of bilingual ability throughout a community. The next five chapters discuss specific techniques for evaluating bilingual ability.

6
Oral Proficiency Testing

The best part of human language, properly so called, is derived from reflection on the acts of the mind itself.

Samuel Taylor Coleridge
Biographia Literaria

6.1 Description

There are several oral proficiency tests in existence. The most well-known is that developed by the Foreign Service Institute (FSI) of the United States Department of State. It dates from the early 1950's and has been altered in various ways since its inception. Although the FSI oral proficiency test is designed and used for the needs of foreign service personnel, it has been modified by other organizations to meet their specific needs.

The most radical modification was done by the American Council of Teachers of Foreign Languages (ACTFL) in the 1970's. They desired to use oral proficiency testing as a means of evaluating students' progress in learning a foreign language in the classroom. The Summer Institute of Linguistics (SIL) has also made modifications in the FSI oral proficiency test in order to evaluate the bilingual ability of people who acquired their second language skills in spheres outside of government service or the classroom (i.e., informally). This variety of the oral proficiency test is called the Second Language Oral Proficiency Evaluation (SLOPE). Since both the FSI and ACTFL oral proficiency tests assume the subjects being evaluated to be literate, neither of these testing procedures was felt to be adequate for the situations where SIL commonly needs to evaluate bilingualism.

Most of the differences between SLOPE and the FSI oral proficiency test were made in order to allow people who are not literate to be evaluated. [8]

Like most methods derived from the FSI oral proficiency test, SLOPE conceives of bilingual ability as ranging from no bilingual ability (Level 0) to bilingual ability equivalent to the ability that educated native speakers have in controlling their mother tongue (Level 5). This yields six base levels (Levels 0, 1, 2, 3, 4, 5). The first five of these base levels also have advanced gradations which are designated by a plus sign (Levels 0+, 1+, 2+, 3+, 4+). The advanced designation is allocated to individuals who, while basically functioning at one of the base levels, sometimes show a level of ability characteristic of the next higher level. Since Level 5 is the evaluation given to someone functioning at the top of the scale (i.e., as an educated native speaker), there is no Level 5+.

SLOPE is also similar to other methods of oral proficiency testing in that it depends on an interview with test subjects as the means of gathering data about their bilingual ability and the final rating is assigned by an evaluator. Most oral proficiency tests depend on rigorous training and constant comparison of evaluations among evaluators in order to reduce the element of subjectivity inherent in such an evaluation process. It remains to be seen whether this will be possible with SLOPE.

The administration of SLOPE requires the skills of three people. One of these people is an evaluator of oral proficiency who is trained according to the standards set forth in Summer Institute of Linguistics 1987. An evaluator, sometimes referred to as the LINGUIST, need not have a great deal of familiarity with the second language. The second person, referred to as the TESTER, must be a mother-tongue speaker of the second language and a skilled conversationalist. The third person, referred to as the ASSISTANT, must be a mother-tongue speaker of the subject's vernacular and also control the second language fairly well. Each interview lasts a minimum of thirty minutes and at least another ten minutes is needed after the interview is completed to do the evaluation. Each interview is recorded, so a tape recorder with a microphone capable of picking up the conversation is needed also.

6.2 Procedures

The interview. The goal of the interview is to elicit a speech sample from the people being interviewed which adequately demonstrates the

---

[8]For a detailed description of SLOPE see Summer Institute of Linguistics 1987. For a description of the FSI oral proficiency test, see Wilds (1975). For an overview of the oral proficiency testing within FSI, see Sollenberger 1978.

Survey on a Shoestring

range of their abilities in the second language. The interview consists of three parts—the first for introduction and warm-up, a second where subjects demonstrate their skill in the second language by relating known information, and a third where subjects demonstrate their ability to use the second language in order to get previously unknown information. All three parts consist of a conversation between a SUBJECT and a TESTER.

During a SLOPE interview the tester must speak to a subject as though the subject were also a mother-tongue speaker of the second language.[9] The speech variety used must not be adjusted in order to make it easier for a subject to understand, unless the subject asks for such modification. The tester is expected to employ as full a range of conversational strategies as is appropriate to the situation.

In the last two parts of the interview, the subject is briefed on what to talk about or what to ask about. The topics are selected by the person administering the test. They are chosen in order to ensure that the subjects have an opportunity to demonstrate their second language ability in a variety of domains, including those which are perhaps not normally domains for second-language use by speakers of the subject's vernacular. The topics are explained to the subject by someone who is a mother-tongue speaker of the subject's vernacular. These briefings usually consist of about five minutes of conversation in the vernacular about topics supplied by the person administering the test. The purpose of the briefings is to ensure that the subject has a number of ideas about possible things to talk about. Each of the three conversational parts of the interview lasts between five and ten minutes.

Evaluating the interview. The task of evaluating the speech sample which has been elicited as a result of the interview falls upon someone who has been trained in SLOPE techniques. This is usually the same person who has trained the tester and the assistant in their roles. In some cases it may be possible to train the tester to be the evaluator.[10] Throughout the interview the evaluator pays careful attention to the speech and body language of the subject. It is helpful if the evaluator is able to distinguish

---

[9]The procedures for conducting a SLOPE evaluation are described in detail in Summer Institute of Linguistics 1987. Anyone considering using SLOPE should read this and be trained in the evaluation procedures by someone who has done it.

[10]If testers are trained to give evaluations of oral proficiency, they should go through the same training procedures necessary for any other evaluator. Care must be taken to ensure the reliability of the scores given by different evaluators. Anyone who is doing evaluations should have first practiced by rating speech samples that have already been rated. Evaluations should only be done on speech samples elicited through an interview in order to ensure that the rating is based on a sample which adequately represents the subject's capabilities.

between the vernacular and the second language, even if neither language is understood. It is usually quite clear whether or not a subject has to struggle in order to produce intelligible utterances in the second language. In the event that the evaluator does not understand the second language, after the interview is complete, the evaluator reviews the tape of the interview with the tester and the assistant and notes their comments on the subject's second language ability. The evaluator then scores the subject's performance in six different areas of competence and awards an overall score in terms of one of the levels mentioned previously.

6.3 Advantages

SLOPE has several advantages that commend it. Apart from observation, it is probably the least intimidating of the various tests of bilingual ability discussed here. The conversational format is markedly less threatening than the prospect of wearing headphones for many potential subjects. SLOPE also gives balanced attention to both the production and comprehension aspects of bilingual ability. In addition it looks at bilingual ability in a comparatively natural context, as it does not depend upon a subject's reaction to recorded speech samples in order to evaluate the subject's production and comprehension abilities in the second language. By allowing individuals to demonstrate their communicative competence, SLOPE is also able to account for second language use in a variety of domains.

SLOPE is likely to be most useful in communities with a wide range of bilingual abilities, or in those in which levels of bilingualism are relatively high. It appears to be one of the few tests with the potential to adequately discriminate among the higher levels of bilingual ability. For this reason SLOPE would also be useful as a technique by which other tests could be calibrated to an oral proficiency scale.

6.4 Disadvantages

The version of oral proficiency testing known as SLOPE is still being field tested. Although SLOPE has some important advantages, it also has some important disadvantages. The test has fairly extensive training requirements compared to other tests. Standardization of the evaluation methodology is a problem in many bilingual evaluations techniques, but SLOPE seems particularly susceptible to the possibility of subjective scoring unless adequate training is available. Steps must also be taken to ensure that reliability in scoring exists among different evaluators, even among evaluators concerned with different second languages. Interviews can take as long as an hour to administer and evaluate. It may take as many as a dozen interviews before a tester and assistant are reliably able to perform their tasks. Because SLOPE takes so much time, it is probably better reserved for those communities which a pilot study has shown to have a high degree of bilingualism.[11]

---

[11]For an overview of the theoretical concerns raised by oral proficiency testing, see Lado (1978), Lantolf and Frawley (1985), and Savignon (1985).

7
Recorded Text Tests

> The cruelest lies are often told in silence.
> Robert Louis Stevenson
> *Virginibus Puerisque*

7.1 Description

This method of evaluating bilingual ability has been adapted from dialect intelligibility tests. A recorded text test consists of a short text spoken by a mother-tongue speaker of the second language being tested. A subject listens to the text one time. The subject then hears the text a second time, with questions about the text interspersed in appropriate places throughout the text. The questions are dubbed into the text following the portion which contains the answer to the question. These questions are in the subject's mother tongue. A test has ten questions. If a subject is unable to respond to a question on the first hearing, no second chance is given. This is standard practice as it is important that every question have the same chance of being answered correctly. Randomly allowing some questions to be played more than once may improve the chances of those questions being answered correctly.[12] Subjects may respond to the question in any language they choose, provided they control that language well enough to respond accurately. The response given by a subject is written down and translated. Care should be taken to ensure that the same responses are translated in the same way.

---

[12] If for some obvious reason the subject did not hear the question (e.g., the subject removes the headphones just as the question is being asked), then a replay is obviously indicated.

The responses given by a subject are compared with a list of responses given by mother-tongue speakers of the second language to the same questions. Those responses given by a subject which differ significantly from those given by mother-tongue speakers of the second language are counted as inappropriate. A percentage score of the appropriate responses is then calculated.

When recorded text tests are used, the levels of bilingual ability are usually expressed by these percentages. An individual who scores high on the test is assumed to be more bilingual than an individual who scores lower. As should be clear from the preceding description, this test measures only comprehension of the second language. A score of 100 percent does not mean that the individual is 'completely' bilingual. It is thought that subjects who are 2+ or higher on the SLOPE scale will usually score 100 percent on a recorded text test. This means that recorded text tests are most useful as pilot tests of the bilingual ability in a community. They are also useful in communities where bilingual ability is not thought to be very high.

The kind of text used in a recorded text test affects the scores obtained. For a dialect intelligibility test a narrative text is used. This is also the kind of text most frequently used when testing bilingualism. See Casad (1974:11) for a description of this kind of text. Grimes (1986a) says that if recorded text testing is used as a means of evaluating bilingualism, texts of several different kinds should be used—narrative, procedural, hortatory, and expository.[13] She also recommends that topics covering several different domains be included. This is especially necessary if recorded text tests are the test being applied to a community which includes some very bilingual people. In some communities it is sufficient to use two texts, one a narrative and the second a nonnarrative expository text. Or the second text could use a variety of the second language that is normally only within the competence of an educated mother-tongue speaker of the second language.

A recorded text test is usually administered by two people. One person controls the tape recorder and another person writes down the responses the subject gives. At least one person needs to have some ability in the mother tongue of the subjects. A single recorded text test takes about ten minutes to administer. Most subjects listen to at least two texts, and sometimes to as many as five. In order to administer the test a recorder with two or three headphones is necessary. In order to prepare the test tapes, two recorders are needed, along with a patch cord in order to dub the tapes. A microphone is needed in order to make the original recordings.

---

[13]Eliciting nonnarrative texts suitable for recorded text testing can be quite difficult in many survey situations.

7.2 Procedures

The basic procedures involved in creating and testing recorded text tests are described in Casad 1974. His discussion focuses primarily on their use in dialect intelligibility testing. Essentially the same procedures are used when recorded text tests are used to evaluate bilingualism.

Obtaining a text. Use one tape for master copies of all the texts that will be needed for a survey. Before recording a text on the master text tape, record a brief 'tag' on the tape which identifies the language, the speaker, the location, the date, and the subject matter of the text. A mother-tongue speaker of the second language should record the text. Explain what kind of material is needed. Some people will wish to write out the text first and read it. This is acceptable if it does not result in an oversimplification of the text, if the style used is acceptable for oral use, and if the speaker is able to read it in a natural manner. Other speakers, either by choice or necessity, will wish to use a strictly oral approach. It may be necessary for a speaker to retell a story a couple of times before a satisfactory version is found. Do not record over previous versions of a story until a better one is recorded! Subsequent attempts at the same story are often worse. Explain to the speakers who are recording texts what their texts will be used for and make sure they understand and agree. This avoids placing the speaker in any of several potentially embarrassing situations, such as describing technical infractions of the law that one of the characters in the text may have committed. It also helps ensure that the text is one which it is culturally appropriate for large numbers of people to hear. The length of the text will vary depending on the material. Usually three minutes of text is more than sufficient.

Once a satisfactory text has been recorded, do a rough transcription of the first twenty or so sentences of the text, or have the speaker do it in a script shared by members of the survey team. In some cases it will be useful to have a transcription in more than one script. An accurate phonetic transcription is not necessary at this point, although it will be useful for the final report. Translate the text both literally (i.e., word-for-word) and idiomatically (i.e., freely). Both translations are usually necessary in order to avoid errors in composing questions about the text. (27) shows possible formats for such transcriptions and translations.

The interlinear single-script format for transcribing texts can be used when everyone involved in the elicitation process uses the same script. The first line of the text is written in the shared script. Beneath this transcription, the gloss for each word (i.e., the literal translation) is written. Beneath the literal

(27) Interlinear Formats for Text Transcriptions

Single Script Format	Double Script Format
1. Transcription Literal Translation Idiomatic Translation	1. Script Transcription Phonetic Transcription Literal Translation Idiomatic Translation
2. Transcription Literal Translation Idiomatic Translation	2. Script Transcription Phonetic Transcription Literal Translation Idiomatic Translation
3. Transcription Literal Translation Idiomatic Translation	3. Script Transcription Phonetic Transcription Literal Translation Idiomatic Translation

translation, the idiomatic translation of the line is written. This process is repeated for the second line of the text, then for the third, and so on.

If everyone involved in the survey does not use the same script, an interlinear double-script format like that in (27) can be used. The first line of the text is written in the local script. Beneath this script transcription, a phonetic transcription is written. Beneath this phonetic transcription, the literal translation is written. Beneath the literal translation, the idiomatic translation of the line is written. This process is repeated for the second line of the text, then for the third, and so on.

Obtaining questions for a text. After the first twenty or so sentences have been transcribed and translated, devise as many questions for each of the twenty sentences as possible. Cover as many semantic areas as possible for each sentence. Casad (1974:12–13) lists the questions presented in (28).

(28)
1. Participant as actor
2. Participant as goal
3. Object as goal
4. Description of condition
5. Description of character
6. Specific Event
7. Ground (or explanation) of event
8. Purpose
9. Result
10. Cause
11. Time
12. Instrument
13. Quantity
14. Quotative
15. Manner
16. Location

Questions should be specific and detailed. For example, use names and nouns rather than pronouns to refer to the characters in the text. "Why did the boy go to Ram Chandra's house?" is a better question than "Why did he go to his house?" Avoid questions that have more than one possible response or which require subjects to deduce an answer from the text. Avoid questions which require either a 'yes' or 'no' response.

When questions have been formulated in this manner, it should be clear whether the first twenty sentences of the text contain enough material for an adequate test. If they do not, transcribe and translate another twenty sentences and repeat the process of making questions for each sentence. It is best if the end of the story coincides with the end of the material used for the test, but not necessary. Similarly, it is possible to use the middle or final part of a text as a test, as long as the material does not depend too heavily on what has gone before. If possible, more than one person should be involved in creating and checking the list of tentative questions.

When several questions have been created for each of twenty sentences of the text, review the questions and select the best fifteen or so. Try to ensure that each question covers a semantic area different from the other questions. Select only one question for each sentence of the text. Try to choose the most detailed and least ambiguous questions. Review these fifteen questions with the person who recorded the text or another mother-tongue speaker of the second language who has heard the text in order to ensure that the questions are appropriate.

When fifteen or so questions have been selected, translate them back into the second language. The translation should be idiomatic and natural, though this may require that several changes be made in the original structure of the question. For example, a question such as: "Why did the boy and his father decide not to steal?" may be translated as "Should the boy and his father decide to stop stealing? Why?" if the structure of the second language requires it. It is not, however, permissible for a question to be changed into one that requires only a 'yes' or 'no' response in the course of the translation.

When the questions have been translated, record them on a tape different from the one used for the text. Use the same tape for all the questions recorded on the survey. Having a separate master question tape will save a lot of rewinding and fast-forwarding when the time comes to make the test tape. Before each set of questions record a brief tag which identifies the language of the questions, the story for which they were made, the speaker, and the date and location of the recording. If possible, use someone besides the speaker who recorded the text to record the questions. If a man recorded the text, then use a woman, or a boy to record the questions. This ensures that the voice quality of the text is different from the voice quality used for the questions. This lessens the chance that the subjects will confuse the text material with the questions. If it is not possible to have a second mother-tongue speaker of the second language record the questions, have the first speaker record the questions at a little louder volume than the text. Record the number of each question first. The number should be recorded in a language understood by the members of the survey team. The number should be followed by the question being asked twice, with a brief pause between the repetitions. Make sure that the person recording the questions knows that they are questions and that the intonation patterns are appropriate.

The test tape. The first item on any test tape should be a short explanation of the test procedure in the mother tongue of the people being tested. The explanation text should be something like that in (29).

(29) This machine is a tape recorder.
It tells stories.
Listen carefully to each story.
After the story, you will hear questions.
When you hear the question, please answer it.
Now, here is the first story...

If the same explanation text will be used several times, it is best to record it on the master text tape. Otherwise it can be recorded directly on to the test tape.

The second item which should be dubbed on to any test tape is a practice test. This practice test consists of a short story and a few questions in the mother tongue of the subjects for whom the test tape is being prepared. An example of a practice test is presented in (30).

(30) My father bought a cow. It cost Rs. 600. One day, as I was milking the cow, the milk spilled on the ground. My mother scolded me for that.

My father bought a cow.
Question: What did his father buy?

It cost Rs. 600.
Question: How much did the cow cost?

One day, as I was milking the cow, the milk spilled on the ground.
Question: What happened to the milk?

My mother scolded me for that.
Question: What did his mother do?

Practice tests are necessary in order to train people in how to take the test. If a subject is unable to respond appropriately to the questions on a

Survey on a Shoestring 79

practice test in the vernacular, there is usually no point in proceeding to the other tests on the test tape with that subject. If there is not a practice test on the tape, the subjects learn how to take the test on the first text on the tape. This is unsatisfactory, as it usually results in the first four or five questions for that text being answered inappropriately, if at all. This artificially lowers the score for that test and skews the overall results. Using a practice test is strongly recommended.

A practice test may be developed in a manner similar to that described above. As an alternative, the same practice story can be translated into each vernacular. If the practice test is translated, care should be taken that the material is culturally appropriate. For the practice test in the example this would mean checking to see if the price of the cow was appropriate for that region, if the use of dairy products was acceptable to the culture of the people who use the vernacular in question, and making sure that the story is told by a person of the appropriate sex. In some communities, milking cows may be a job that belongs exclusively to one or the other of the sexes.

The third item to be recorded on a test tape is the first of the texts to be tested on the subjects. This text should always be in the vernacular of the subjects for whom the tape is intended. All subjects are first tested on a text in their own language. This is done for two reasons. The first reason is that it builds up the confidence of the subject. If the first test that subjects hear is in their own vernacular, this often helps to overcome their doubts about participating in the testing procedure.

The second reason is that having a score for each subject in their vernacular serves as a control for that subject. Subjects who have scored well on a text in their vernacular but who subsequently score low on a text in a different language demonstrate a difference in their ability to understand the two languages. If, however, subjects score low on the text in the vernacular as well as on subsequent tests, it is clear that these subjects have not mastered the test procedures and the test is invalid for those subjects. Usually, subjects who cannot score 70 percent on the test in the their own vernacular are not tested with texts from other dialects or languages.

After the vernacular text, any other tests which are intended for a group of subjects may be dubbed onto the test tape. It is a good idea to alternate those texts expected to be 'easier' with those expected to be 'difficult' in order to avoid frustrating a subject before the tests are complete.

When both a text and the questions for that text have been recorded, they can be dubbed onto a test tape. Dubbing is a simple procedure which requires two tape recorders, preferably both with pause buttons on them, and a patch cord to connect them. The recorder used to play the master tapes may be called the source machine and the recorder with the test tape may be called the target machine. Put the master text tape in the source machine and record the entire story onto the test tape in the target machine. Then rewind the tape in the source machine to the beginning of the text. Now record the first portion of the master text on the test tape in the target machine. A portion consists of that part of the text which contains the answer to a question. A portion is usually one sentence long, but may consist of several sentences in some cases. When the first portion has been recorded on the test tape, take the master text tape out of the source machine and put in the master question tape. Record the first question on the test tape. Do not record the question number. Since each question has been recorded twice on the master question tape, it is possible to take the best of the two utterances. Leave a one second pause on the test tape after the question has been recorded. Now take the master question tape out of the source machine and put the master text tape back in. Record the second portion of the text onto the test tape. Again, take out the master text tape and put in the master question tape and record the second question onto the test tape. Leave a one second pause on the test tape and repeat this process for each of the fifteen or so questions.

Control test. Just as the subjects taking recorded text tests need to take a control test in their own vernacular, each test should be control tested with a population of mother-tongue speakers of that language. This helps ensure that the test is properly designed. In particular, the fifteen or so questions that have been formulated for a text need to be checked in order to make sure that the person who designed the test understood the text in the same way that the text is understood by mother-tongue speakers of that language. Even if the questions were formulated by a mother-tongue speaker of the language used for the text, it is still necessary to pilot test the test on a sample of mother-tongue speakers of that language.

When questions have been formulated for a text, and the test tape has been created following the procedures described in the previous section, the test tape should be played for ten mother-tongue speakers of the language used in the text. As mentioned previously, questions are always to be in the vernacular of the subjects being tested. In this case that means that the questions and the text are in the same language. The responses given by the ten subjects should be written down without making an immediate judgment as to whether they are appropriate or inappropriate.

When ten people have been tested, make a list of all the responses that were given for each question. By each response note how many times that response was given. Some of the responses will not agree with those that

Survey on a Shoestring

were expected. Go over the text again and see if those responses make more sense than the responses that were expected. Make a special note of those questions for which there are two or more possible responses and those questions to which it seems impossible to respond with any degree of consistency with the text. These questions are candidates for elimination from the test.

Evaluating the questions. After a text has been control tested according to the procedures described in the previous section, a decision must be made about which of the fifteen or so questions will be retained. The final form of the test should have ten questions. First eliminate those questions which were responded to inappropriately more than twice. If there are more than ten questions still remaining, eliminate any of those still remaining which have more than one response. (It is sometimes advisable to retain a question with multiple responses, as long as it is clear that the different responses are derived from the text.) If there are still more than ten questions left, eliminate those which duplicate a semantic category covered by another question. If there are still more than ten questions, eliminate those which were answered inappropriately more than once or those which seemed most frequently misunderstood.

When all but ten questions have been eliminated, tabulate each person's score and calculate the average (mean) for the scores. For the test to be usable, this score should be 90 percent or higher. If the average score is lower than 90 percent, it means too many of the questions were answered inappropriately too frequently for the test to be a reliable instrument. If the average score is above 90 percent, the test is usable. Ideally the average score should be 100 percent. Since surveys are often done in a less than ideal world of momentary (and longer) distractions caused by boredom, crying children, pots boiling over, honking horns, buses leaving, and barking dogs, scores as low as 90 percent on a control test are acceptable. If the score is lower than 90 percent when it has been administered to mother-tongue speakers of the language in question, it can hardly be used as a test of bilingual ability with subjects for whom that language is a second language.

Administering the test. When a test has been control tested, it may then be added to the list of tests to be administered to subjects who are second-language speakers of that language. As has been mentioned previously, the questions must be translated into the vernacular of the people being tested. The subjects must also have heard an explanation text and a practice test in their own language, as well as having passed a recorded text test in their own language. Ideally they should score 100 percent on recorded text tests in their own language. In fact scores sometimes range from 70 percent to

100 percent. If a subject scores below 70 percent on the vernacular, there is usually no point in proceeding with the remaining tests.

When all the recorded text tests have been control tested and dubbed on a test tape, bilingualism testing can then proceed. The people tested should be selected according to the sample developed on the basis of the demographic profile. Record the responses each subject gives on a separate page in a notebook. The responses may be written either in the language in which they were given, or they may be translated on the spot. If they are translated, however, care should be taken to ensure that the same response is translated the same way when it is given by different subjects, and also that different translators are translating the same response the same way. It is probably best not to make any attempt to evaluate the subject's responses as appropriate or inappropriate until all the people in the sample have been tested. This is especially true if more than one person is involved in evaluating the responses. Use one of the front pages of the notebook to keep track of the kinds of people who have already been tested. On this page draw a chart with labels similar to those in (31). When a subject has completed the test schedule, write the page number which has those results in the appropriate box in the chart.

In many cases, the people being tested will be people for whom the census information has already been collected. If this is the case, then at the top of the page in the notebook which contains that subject's test results write the page number and notebook in which that subject's census information may be found. If the subject is someone on whom the census information has not previously been collected, the census information needs to be taken at the time of the test and kept with that subject's test results.

Evaluating the test results. When the sample is complete or nearly complete, the evaluation of the responses given by the subjects can begin. Those responses which clearly match those given by the subjects of the control test for that text are appropriate. Those responses which indicate that the subject did not understand the text (e.g., silence, "I don't know," "It didn't say," etc.) may be counted as inappropriate. Many responses will fall in between these two extremes and must be decided upon as they occur. Most often responses of this nature are those which, while derived from the text, do not match those given by any of the subjects in the control test. Such responses are generally counted as inappropriate as they usually indicate a misunderstanding of the text. In a few cases, however, the responses indicate a quite ingenious understanding of the text and may be counted as appropriate. It is important to maintain consistency in evaluating responses and it is recommended that all the responses for a single test be evaluated by one person in a single sitting. When the

Survey on a Shoestring 83

evaluation is complete, a percentage score of the appropriate responses may then be assigned to the different tests of each subject. These scores should be written on the same page where the subjects' responses to the test questions were written. In addition, each response should be marked as to whether it was judged to be inappropriate or not. This is because the test will probably be used again at some future date and it is desirable to maintain a record of how various responses were evaluated.

When the evaluations of a test are complete, the scores may be transferred to another page in the notebook and organized according to the demographic categories in the sample. (31) gives an example with hypothetical scores on a bilingualism recorded text test. This table assumes a sample with two variables (sex and education) and two values for each variable; other samples will vary from this depending on the situations.

(31) Individual Scores on Bilingualism Recorded Text Test

	Men		Women		
	70	40	80		
	70	40	80		Average (mean) score: 72
Uneducated	60	40	70		Standard deviation: 19
	60		50		Sample size: 33
	50		40		
	100	90	100	90	
	100	90	100	90	
Educated	100	80	90	90	
	100	80	90	80	
	100	70	90	80	

In (31) the average score for the entire sample is given. However, the average score for an entire sample is not very useful in a bilingualism sample as it says nothing about the range of scores that exist within the sample. That the range is quite wide is shown by the fact that the standard deviation is quite high.

The average score for each cell in the matrix should be calculated, as well as the standard deviation, yielding a chart like that in (32).

From a chart like (32) it is clear that the educated portion of the sample is the more bilingual. Among the uneducated portion of the sample women are more bilingual than men, but education evens out this advantage. The standard deviation is still relatively high for uneducated women. This indicates that there is a wide range of scores among uneducated women. A wide range of scores in any particular category usually means that there is still another

(32) Average Scores on Bilingualism Recorded Text Test

	Men	Women
Uneducated	X = 54 s = 13 N = 8	X = 64 s = 18 N = 5
Educated	X = 91 s = 11 N = 10	X = 90 s = 11 N = 10

X = Average score (mean): 72
s = Standard deviation: 19
N = Sample size: 33

variable affecting the scores which the sample has not taken into account. In this case, it might be that the older uneducated women scored higher, while the younger uneducated women scored lower. If the census information for the subjects is checked and it is discovered that the three uneducated women who scored the seventy and the eighties are older than the women who scored the forty and the fifty, then this hypothesis would hold promise, but the sample of uneducated women is too small to confirm or deny it. At least three more younger uneducated women would have to be tested and two more older uneducated women. A high standard deviation in recorded text testing almost always means that the sample has not accounted for all the variables which are influencing bilingualism.

7.3 Advantages

Recorded text testing has two practical advantages. The first is that the procedure is one that is relatively easy to train researchers to carry out. After trainees have seen the test administered a few times, they are usually able to administer the test themselves. Making the test tapes is more difficult than just testing them, but not insurmountably so.

The second practical advantage of recorded text testing is that it is relatively quick. It takes two people a minimum of twenty minutes to test one subject. Forty minutes is usually the maximum amount of time needed for testing one subject. The actual amount of time depends on how many tests are being used.

There are two situations where recorded text testing is most useful. The first is in pilot testing for bilingualism. In deciding how important it is to do a more thorough bilingualism study in a particular community, it is often helpful to have some idea of how bilingual a community is. Such knowledge is also helpful in deciding what kinds of tests to use in order to

Survey on a Shoestring

measure bilingualism. A pilot test of bilingual ability can be done on the same sample that is used for dialect intelligibility studies early in the survey. If that sample (usually only ten people) scores quite well on a recorded text test in the second language, then a fairly extensive study of bilingual ability with careful sampling is probably necessary. If scores on the recorded text test are low, it is probably safe to assume that bilingual ability in the community in that language is not very great and there is no need for an extensive study of bilingualism.

Recorded text testing is also useful in situations where the range of bilingual ability is not wide and limited to the lower end of the scale (i.e., Level 2+ and below). If it is suspected that most of a community has little ability in the second language, then recorded text testing, used with careful sampling techniques, can be helpful in proving or disproving that hypothesis. Of course, if it is disproved, then more information is needed on those parts of the sample which scored the highest on the recorded text test. This is one reason why it is always good to use two different tests in combination when investigating bilingualism.

7.4 Disadvantages

There are two practical disadvantages to recorded text testing. The first is that the procedure, involving, as it does, technology and cultural assumptions foreign to many communities, can be somewhat intimidating to naive subjects. It is not unusual for individuals to refuse to participate in the tests because they do not wish to put on a pair of headphones. This can tend to skew a sample towards those most familiar with foreign ideas (and people), which in many communities is also likely to be the most bilingual part of the population. Careful sampling, while partially rectifying this, cannot completely erase the effects of such skewing. Unfortunately, this is a problem with all bilingualism tests to some degree.

The second practical problem with recorded text testing is that it is certainly not a direct measure of anything besides comprehension. If bilingual ability is low, this is probably not a great drawback. However, bilingual ability is much more than ability to comprehend what is said in the second language. Recorded text testing offers no indication as to how well a subject is able to use the second language, especially in communities with a higher degree of bilingualism.

Recorded text testing is probably less useful in communities with a wide range of bilingual ability. The test will differentiate at the lower end of the scale, but probably cannot differentiate accurately at the higher end.

8
Observation

> Monkeys, who very sensibly refrain from speech, lest they should be set to earn their livings.
>
> Kenneth Grahame
> *Lusisiti Satis*

8.1 Description

Most of the methods of evaluating bilingual ability discussed here are QUANTITATIVE. A quantitative study normally obtains data from questionnaires or from behavior exhibited in controlled situations (e.g., a test). They conceive of bilingual ability as something that can be possessed in a certain amount and express that amount in terms of numbers. Observation, however, is a QUALITATIVE tool. Qualitative methods gather data based on uncontrolled, or 'normal', behavior. They seek not to describe 'how much' bilingualism exists, but rather the kind of phenomenon it is. Both kinds of information are important and work together to give a complete picture of bilingualism in a community. To draw an analogy from physiology, a quantitative measure of the volume of blood in the system of a healthy adult human who is six feet tall and weighs 175 pounds is about 6,000 cc. It would be wrong to assume that a person with more blood is more healthy and a person with less blood is less healthy. The normal volume of blood for someone who is five foot three inches tall and weighs 110 pounds is about 4,000 cc. Weight, height, and volume of blood are all quantitative measures. Observation seeks to describe what it is that blood does in the system. Observation examines the functions of the blood as it carries oxygen and nutrients to the different parts of the body, and carries away waste material. It is the qualitative information that is gained from observation that falsifies the conclusion that a person is healthier the more blood there is in the system. Qualitative information injects a note of reality into the somewhat abstruse world of numbers.

There is no sense in collecting data on how bilingual an individual or community is unless it is known what is done with the second language. It is as though bilingual ability were substituted for blood in the physiological example. Quantitative measures may be able to discover the 'amount' of bilingualism, and correlate that with other factors such as sex and education. But it is also necessary to know what the second language is used for in order to understand why communities or individuals are as bilingual as they are.

Grimes 1988a mentions a survey in which recorded text testing was done among several languages. On the test for one language, scores of speakers of all the languages were consistently above 90 percent. Mother-tongue speakers of that widely-understood language, however, only scored between 25 percent and 38 percent on the tests in the other languages. The surveyors, on the basis of this quantitative data, drew the erroneous conclusion that the other languages were only dialects of the one language on which everyone scored 95 percent. Other studies showed that a high incidence of bilingualism in the widely-understood language accounted for the high scores in that language. In a similar case, it was the observation that the language being tested was from the market center of the area, and therefore well known to those individuals who frequented the market, that corrected a similar, erroneous interpretation of qualitative data.

OBSERVATION is a critically important tool in any bilingualism study. In the physiological analogy, it was noted that weight and height were the two criteria which correlated most closely with volume of blood. An attempt could be made to correlate any number of other factors with volume of blood. Some, such as hair color or number of teeth, would be extraneous. Others, such as lung volume or the diameter of the aorta, might not be so obviously extraneous. It is only because observation has discovered what the body uses blood for that it is possible to understand why it should correlate with weight and size. Similarly, observation in a bilingualism study helps determine what social characteristics are likely to be important in understanding the variables that influence bilingualism.

In another survey, one of the researchers noticed that people who lived close to the one road through the valley were able to talk much more easily to mother-tongue speakers of the second language and were much more likely to participate in affairs apart from those which concerned their own linguistic community. Because of this initial observation, distance from the road was included as one of the variables which were checked for correlation with bilingual ability. The correlation showed that the closer people lived to the road, the more likely they were to be bilingual. Results which otherwise would have been anomalous were accounted for because of this initial observation.

8.2 Procedures

Qualitative methods have long been used in social science research, particularly by anthropologists. Two will be discussed here—PARTICIPANT OBSERVATION and ETHNOGRAPHIC INTERVIEWING.[14]

Participant observation. Participant observation is basically a learning skill. To the old saying about "monkey see, monkey do," might be added "monkey do, and monkey know why." Applied as a research tool participant observation claims "to give privileged access to meanings through the researcher's empathetic sharing of experience in the worlds he or she studies" (Platt 1983:393).

The first step in participant observation is gaining the acceptance of the community. Participant observation is so named because the observation is done from the viewpoint of a participant in the life of the community, not because the researcher is the participant being observed by the community. The presence of the researcher in the community must become familiar and natural in the eyes of the members of the community. It is only as the researcher becomes accepted in the community that people begin to behave in an unselfconscious manner in the presence of the researcher. In some ways, the best participant observer is a person who was born and raised in the community. Most researchers will not have this advantage, but the more frequently they are seen by members of the community, the more quickly a wider range of behavior may be observed.

There is no strict dividing line between self-conscious and unselfconscious behavior. All behavior is more or less self-conscious. For this reason useful observations can begin to be made right from the first day in the community. At the very least, note can be taken of the variety of languages that are used in attempting to communicate with a stranger. The more frequently the researcher is with the people of the community under study, the sooner the researcher's presence ceases to become an object of comment.

---

[14]Spradley 1980 gives a detailed description of participant observation, and Spradley 1979 gives a similarly detailed discussion of ethnographic interviewing. For an example of how these might be applied in the context of a sociolinguistic survey, see Keller 1986.

One key to successful participant observation is attention to detail. The observer should note not just the frequency of second-language use, but also the context of the speech act. Fishman's (1965) question: "Who speaks what language to whom and when?" is relevant at the very least. An important part of participant observation is recording the events which have been observed. If it is impractical to write down notes immediately after an event is observed, at the very least a journal can be kept recording the day's observations. For many people, keeping a journal is a useful discipline which forces them to pay closer attention to what is going on around them in order to have something to write about.

Ethnographic interviews. ETHNOGRAPHY is the art of writing about a people and their culture as they themselves see it. CULTURE is understood by ethnographers to be the rules for generating and interpreting social behavior. An ETHNOGRAPHIC INTERVIEW is a conversation designed to elicit these rules. If participant observation is learning through doing, then ethnographic interviewing is learning through talking. The two methods are not, of course, mutually exclusive.

In ethnographic interviewing, data is collected in a series of conversations between the researcher and a member of the community being investigated. These conversations are recorded and transcribed for analysis. Analysis involves discovering more questions to be asked in the next conversation. The point of the conversations is to enable the researcher to understand the world view of the community being studied. The conversations are therefore open-ended. Researchers have in mind a topic which they wish to investigate, and come to the conversation with questions designed to elicit information on that topic, but researchers must avoid placing an alien interpretive grid on what is said. The point of the exercise is to discover the community's interpretive grid as it is understood by a member of that community.

Three kinds of questions are used in ethnographic interviewing: DESCRIPTIVE, STRUCTURAL and CONTRASTIVE. Bipolar questions and 'why' questions are not very useful in ethnographic interviews. 'Why' questions tend to be unanswerable and bipolar questions tend to impose the researcher's interpretive framework on the data.

DESCRIPTIVE QUESTIONS are designed to elicit detail about an event, institution, idea, or object. 'What,' 'when,' and 'where' questions are all descriptive. For example, if an American primary school student was being interviewed in order to discover how students think about time, descriptive questions might be used to find out that time consists of a day followed by a night; that objects called clocks, watches, and calendars help measure time; that calendars and clocks are usually found hanging on walls.

STRUCTURAL QUESTIONS are used to discover the relationships between events, institutions, ideas, or objects. Since many components of human behavior are hierarchically organized, structural questions are also used to investigate hierarchical relationships. In the previous example, structural questions might be used to elicit the facts that days are grouped into weeks and weeks into months; that there were two different kinds of days—school days and holidays; that holidays could be further subdivided into weekends and special holidays; that examples of special holidays are Christmas, Thanksgiving, and Spring Break.

CONTRASTIVE QUESTIONS are used to elicit differences and similarities between the different components of events, institutions, ideas, or objects, especially between components that exist on the same level of a hierarchy. Contrastive questions are used to discover how a member of a community defines the events, institutions, ideas, and objects that are familiar to the community. In the previous example contrastive questions might be used to discover that calendars measure periods of time longer than a day, while clocks and watches measure periods of time shorter than a day; that clocks are found on walls and are items of furniture, while watches are found on wrists and are items of jewelry.

When used to investigate multilingualism, ethnographic interviews are must useful in helping a researcher discover how the community thinks about language. For instance structural and descriptive questions which are designed to discover what languages are used by what kinds of people can often be useful in identifying variables which correlate with various degrees of bilingual ability. Descriptive and contrastive questions designed to discover how a community thinks about ability in a second language help identify levels of bilingualism which are relevant to the community being studied.

8.3 Advantages

When done properly, observation and ethnographic interviewing can yield data available from no other source. Qualitative methods such as these help to understand how quantitative data should be interpreted. In addition, they can help focus quantitative research on those areas most likely to be profitable.

8.4 Disadvantages

Qualitative methods are enormously time-consuming. For participant observation to cover reliably all the situations of interest means that the observer needs to spend hours in the context where the observations are being made. A great deal of that time will not be of immediate benefit to the current project. For best results, ethnographic interviewing should be done in the vernacular of the people being interviewed. Participant observation is also greatly facilitated if the observer is able to understand what is being said all around. Most survey projects do not allow enough time for these techniques to be used for maximum effect.

9
Sentence Repetition Tests

> Oh, speak again, bright angel...
> William Shakespeare
> *Romeo and Juliet*

9.1 Description

A sentence repetition test consists of a set of carefully selected sentences recorded on tape in the second language. These sentences are each played once for each individual subject. After hearing a sentence subjects have an opportunity to repeat it exactly as they heard it. The evaluator scores the subjects' mimicry on a four point scale (0–3), according to how closely s/he imitated the example on the tape. A subject's score is usually expressed as the total number of points awarded. The higher the score the higher the subject's bilingual ability is assumed to be.

Research in speech pathology and psycholinguistics forms the theoretical background for sentence repetition tests. Casad (1974:88) mentions that psycholinguistics has demonstrated a correlation between ability to mimic sentences and control of grammatical and phonological structure. Norman (1976) says that the average adult capacity for remembering unrelated words is seven, plus or minus two. Radloff (To appear) maintains that this means that for individuals to be able to consistently repeat utterances consisting of more than nine words, they must have some way of structuring them into larger meaningful units.

In speech pathology, sentence repetition tests are used for screening children in order to find those who are not acquiring basic language abilities in their mother tongue as fast as their peers. Experience in the phonetics classroom has shown, however, that individuals vary in their ability to mimic phrases they do not understand. An attempt to control for this is made by limiting the number of opportunities a subject has to hear a sentence.

The sentence repetition test is not a direct measure of bilingual ability. At most it is a direct measure of the subject's production skills in the second language. It is assumed that production skills correlate with comprehension and other language skills, but this correlation has not been demonstrated at very high levels of bilingualism. Indeed, the fact that sentence repetition tests were developed for use with children acquiring basic language skills indicates that they may be more valid at lower levels than at those requiring equivalence to an educated mother-tongue speaker.

It takes about fifteen minutes to administer a sentence repetition test to one person. A recorder and headphones are the only equipment needed to administer the test. If the subject's performance on the test is to be recorded, a second recorder is also needed.

9.2 Procedures

The procedure for constructing, administering and scoring sentence repetition tests may be found in Radloff (To appear). This section briefly summarizes what may be found there in much greater detail.

Constructing a sentence repetition test. The first step in constructing a sentence repetition test is to elicit the sentences that will make up the test. These are drawn from natural texts of various types elicited from mother-tongue speakers of the second language. A variety of sentences should be selected from the natural texts, using such criteria as length and complexity of sentences, as well as domain and register. No more than fifty sentences are to be selected. These fifty sentences are then rerecorded and played for a small number of mother-tongue speakers of the second language in order to get their subjective reaction to the appropriateness and naturalness of the sentences. Any sentences which they disapprove of are eliminated from the corpus.

The sentences that remain are then pilot tested on subjects with a variety of abilities in the second language. At least fifty people should hear the sentences. Some attention should be paid to testing a representative sample of people who use the language being tested; it seems necessary to include at least five of each of the following categories: educated mother-tongue speakers of the second language, people who are mother-tongue speakers of the second language but who have never been to school, people of only marginal ability in the second language, and people with no ability in the second language. It would also seem necessary for all the individuals in this sample who are not mother-tongue speakers of the second language to be mother-tongue speakers of the same vernacular. An individual whose mother tongue is closely related to the second language would probably have an easier time in mimicking the sentences than someone whose mother tongue belongs to a completely different language family. In order to control for this, it seems necessary to have the pilot test involve only speakers of the same mother tongue. The difficulty with this is that the difficulty levels for each sentence are then calculated with regard to speakers of one particular vernacular. It is not certain whether this will affect the results significantly, but it seems likely to. The effect may be so great as to require different versions of each test to be developed for different combinations of vernaculars and second languages.

When fifty people have taken the pilot test and their responses have been scored, a discrimination index and a difficulty level are assigned to each sentence, based on the performance of subjects on that sentence. A sentence with a favorable discrimination index is one which those who performed well repeated successfully and those who performed poorly did not repeat successfully. The final form of the test should include sentences with a variety of difficulty levels, but only those sentences with favorable discrimination indices. Using these difficulty levels certain sentences are determined to be more discriminating than others and these are retained for the final version of the test, which is now ready to be administered.

Test administration. Test administration is a fairly simple matter which consists of having both the subject and the evaluator listening to the sentences. Before the test begins, the procedure is explained in the subject's mother tongue. The subject has a chance to practice mimicking a few practice sentences in the second language.

Each sentence in the test is played and the evaluator notes the way the subject repeats the sentence. Errors may be significant pronunciation mistakes (i.e those which alter meaning), word transpositions, word substitutions, omissions, additions, etc. If the mimicry is exact on the first try, three points are awarded for that sentence. If there is one error, two points are awarded. If two errors occur, then only one point is awarded, and if there are three or more errors, then no points are awarded for that sentence.

9.3 Advantages

Sentence repetition tests are simple and quick to administer. A sentence repetition test which has been reliably calibrated to another bilingualism evaluation method offers the opportunity of quickly evaluating very large samples. Further field testing should demonstrate whether or not sentence repetition tests can distinguish among the higher levels of bilingualism, but they are, at the least, useful in communities where there is not a high degree of bilingualism, or as a pilot test to get an initial indication of what kind of bilingualism study needs to be done.

9.4 Disadvantages

The sentence repetition test appears to be a measure of only one aspect of bilingual ability. An individual's ability to accurately repeat a sentence in the second language is assumed to indicate how much is understood and how capable the subject is in using the second language. The validity of this assumption remains to be convincingly demonstrated. Like other measures of bilingual ability, sentence repetition tests may not adequately distinguish among higher levels of bilingualism and should be used in conjunction with another test.

Another problem with sentence repetition tests is calibration across languages. The same score on sentence repetition tests in two different languages is likely to mean different things. If the sentence repetition test is recalibrated for speakers of each vernacular, it should be reliable for those speakers, in the sense that it will rank subjects along a continuum of ability. It is not certain that this will be the same continuum of ability as that for speakers of a different vernacular.

10
Self-evaluation Questionnaires

> Unlearned, he knew no schoolman's subtle art,
> No language, but the language of the heart.
>
> Alexander Pope, 1734
> *Prologue to the Imitations of Horace.*

10.1 Description

Self-evaluation questionnaires are sometimes called 'Can you do this? questionnaires' because they characteristically inquire about subjects' perceptions of their ability to accomplish a certain task in the second language. Certain of these tasks are regarded as more complex than other tasks. For example, most self-evaluation questionnaires regard the use of the second language in the purchase of a bus ticket to be a fairly simple task. Interpreting a speech in the second language into the vernacular for the benefit of other members of the community who do not understand the second language is a more complex task. If a subject reported himself to be capable of performing the more complex tasks in the second language, that subject is evaluated as more bilingual than a subject who reported himself not able to perform the more complex task.

A self-evaluation questionnaire generally consists of between fifteen and twenty-five questions. Self-evaluation questionnaires are usually derived from the FSI self-evaluation test in Adams and Frith (1979). The example in this section comes from Grimes (1986a:24–26). Other examples of such questionnaires may be found in Quakenbush (1986:269–71) and Brewster and Brewster (1976:374–76). Each question is associated with one of the Language Skill Level Descriptions of the Interagency Language

Roundtable (ILR). Results from self-evaluation questionnaires are usually given in terms of these language skill level descriptions.

In working with preliterate or semiliterate communities, or with communities with a different cultural background than that envisioned by the ILR, it is usually necessary to modify and adapt these questions to the local situation. In other words, the contextualization of a self-evaluation questionnaire to a community is usually necessary. The kinds of changes necessary for this contextualization usually become obvious in the process of translating the questions into the vernacular of the community to be evaluated.

The questions on a self-evaluation questionnaire are all designed to be answered either 'Yes' or 'No'. For most questions, a yes answer is taken to indicate a greater degree of bilingual ability (e.g., "Can you buy a bus ticket using the second language?"). For some questions, however, a no answer indicates a greater degree of bilingualism (e.g., "Do people laugh at the way you speak the second language?"). If an answer indicates a greater degree of bilingual ability, it is referred to as a positive answer, regardless of whether 'yes' or 'no.' Similarly, an answer which indicates a lesser degree of bilingual ability is called a negative answer, again regardless of whether it was actually a 'yes' or a 'no.'

Self-evaluation questionnaires require little technology other than paper and pen. The questions on the questionnaire are asked in the vernacular of the community being investigated, so it is necessary to have someone who can speak the vernacular ask the questions and interpret the answers. Once a self-evaluation questionnaire has been developed and pilot tested it takes about five minutes to administer it to one person.

10.2 Procedures

Self-evaluation questionnaires are described in Grimes (1986a). She recommends that they not be used as the sole tool for evaluating bilingualism in a survey. For an example of how they can be used on a survey, see Quakenbush (1986). He used a self-evaluation questionnaire along with an oral proficiency test in his study of bilingualism among the Agutaynen of Palawan in the Philippines. Stahl (1986) describes the use of self-evaluation questionnaires in tandem with recorded text tests.

Contextualizing a questionnaire. Before a self-evaluation questionnaire can be used it must first be made to fit the local situation. Sometimes the contextualization involves little more than translating the self-evaluation questionnaire into the vernacular of the community where bilingualism is being studied. Other times the questions on the questionnaire have to be quite radically modified. In either case, the list of questions should be thoroughly checked with a native speaker of the vernacular before it is pilot tested.

The most common kind of change in the questions (apart from the structural changes commonly made in any sort of translation process) is to make them more specific. The questions given in Quakenbush (1986) or Grimes (1986a) are couched in general terms. Two problems arise from this. Quite often when such general questions are translated and asked, no response is given by the subject. This is sometimes merely a translation problem. At other times it seems that the question is framed in such general terms that the subject cannot imagine a situation that fits the question.

The other problem arises when a response is given. Different subjects can often imagine different situations based on the same general question. For example, a question like: "Are you afraid that you will misunderstand information given to you (in the second language)?" can as easily be construed to refer to a doctor's advice as to information given by an employer on how to perform a given task. If subjects respond to the questions on the basis of differently imagined social situations, this has the potential of seriously affecting the reliability of the questionnaire results. In discussing this problem, Quakenbush recommends making the questionnaire more specific and says:

> Although this would result in slightly less standardization in the questionnaire, it would ensure that for these particular questions respondents within each location would have the same referent in mind (1986:229–30).

The changes that Quakenbush has in mind with regard to his self-evaluation questionnaire are minor compared to the changes that sometimes have to be made. It is doubtful that standardization can be retained for self-evaluation questionnaires contextualized for different vernaculars. The questionnaire below exemplifies the sorts of changes that often have to be made in contextualizing a self-evaluation questionnaire.

Question 1
Original: Can you tell someone how to get from here to the nearest school or church?
Contextualized: If someone asks you in Oriya, "How is the way to the store?" can you tell him or not?

Question 2
Original: Can you ask and tell the time of the day, day of the week, date?
Contextualized: Can you ask and tell the time of day and day of the week in Oriya?

Question 3
Original: Can you buy food in the market at a just price?
Contextualized: There is one Oriya-speaking merchant. He speaks only Oriya. If you go to him for salt and chili can you pay the correct amount, without giving too much?

Question 4
Original: Can you buy a needed item of clothing or a bus or train ticket?
Contextualized: There is a cloth merchant. He speaks only Oriya. Can you go to him and buy cloth for the correct price, without giving too much money?

Question 5
Original: Can you understand and respond correctly to questions about where you are from, your marital status, occupation, date and place of birth?
Contextualized: Can you tell where you live and who your father is in Oriya?

Question 6
Original: Can you describe your present or most recent job or activity in detail?
Contextualized: Can you tell about what crops you planted and how good they were in Oriya?

Question 7
Original: Can you give detailed information about your family, your house, the weather today?
Contextualized: Can you tell about the members of your family and how you built your house in Oriya?

Question 8
Original: Can you hire someone to work for you and arrange details such as salary, qualifications, hours, specific duties?
Contextualized: You are going for work on the coffee plantations. The supervisor is an Oriya man. If he does not pay you the correct amount, can you ask for it in Oriya? If he tells you to do some work in Oriya, can you understand him?

Survey on a Shoestring 101

Question 9
Original: Can you give a brief story of your life and tell of immediate plans and hopes?
Contextualized: Omitted.

Question 10
Original: Can you describe your home area, giving climate, terrain, types of plants and animals, crops, products made there, peoples and languages?
Contextualized: Can you describe in Oriya the different kinds of people who live in Araku, what work they do, and what their languages sound like?

Question 11
Original: Can you describe what types of leaders you have and what each one does in leading the people? Or can you describe the way children are taught what they need to know to become adults?
Contextualized: Can you tell in Oriya what someone should do if they get a fever?

Question 12
Original: Can you describe why you do the job the way you do?
Contextualized: Can you tell in Oriya on which day to plant seeds and when to harvest?

Question 13
Original: Do you sometimes find yourself not being able to say something in the language?
Contextualized: When you speak Oriya and (the language) is not coming, do you have to be quiet?

Question 14
Original: Do you find it difficult to follow and contribute to a conversation among native speakers who try to include you in their talk?
Contextualized: If Oriya-speaking people want to talk about politics with you, are you able to?

Question 15
Original: Are you afraid that you will misunderstand information given to you?
Contextualized: If you take your child to an Oriya-speaking doctor and he tells you what medicine your child needs to become better and what food you should not give, can you understand him?

Question 16
Original: Can you speak to a group of leaders about your work and be sure you are communicating what you want to without obviously amusing or irritating them by your use of the language?
Contextualized: If you make a mistake while speaking Oriya, do people laugh?

Question 17
> Original: Can you defend your beliefs or those of your people against criticism from someone else?
> Contextualized: If Oriya-speaking people (verbally) fight (with your people) can you return hard (words) in Oriya?

Question 18
> Original: Can you cope as far as language is concerned with such difficult circumstances as a needed house repair, a mistaken encounter with a policeman, a serious social mistake by a friend?
> Contextualized: If your cow gets into the cornfield of an Oriya man and he asks for money for the crop eaten, can you settle the issue?

Question 19
> Original: Can you follow an argument on some social topic?
> Contextualized: If two men are arguing in Oriya about a land boundary, can you follow the argument?

Question 20
> Original: Can you change the way you talk, depending on whether you are talking to educated people, close friends, those who work for you?
> Contextualized: Can you speak to respected people, with ladies, and with children in Oriya?

Question 21
> Original: Can you serve as an informal interpreter for a leader from your mother-tongue group who may not be able to speak the second language very well?
> Contextualized: If an Oriya-speaking M.L.A. comes and speaks to you can you tell the meaning in Konda to all others?

Question 22
> Original: Do you almost never make a mistake?
> Contextualized: Do you ever make a mistake when you speak Oriya?

Question 23
> Original: In discussions on all subjects, are your words always appropriate and exact enough to enable you to convey your exact meaning?
> Contextualized: Do you speak Oriya well?

Question 24
> Original: Can you figure prices in your head in the language without slowing down?
> Contextualized: Omitted.

Question 25
> Original: Can you use as many words in the language as in your language?
> Contextualized: Can you speak Oriya like an Oriya person?

After a self-evaluation questionnaire has been contextualized with the help of a mother-tongue speaker of the community vernacular, it must be pilot tested. Pilot testing consists of a trial run of the questionnaire on a small sample. It is done in order to gauge the suitability of the questions. Questions which are shown during the pilot test to be offensive, confusing, or which are incapable of being answered are either modified to take care of the problem or dropped from the questionnaire. The final form of the self-evaluation questionnaire should have at least three questions for each of the ILR language skill levels from one to five.

Administering a questionnaire. Once a self-evaluation questionnaire has been contextualized and pilot tested, administering it to the sample is a fairly straightforward process. As with other test procedures, it is important to keep track of the relevant census information on each subject. Answers to the questions may be written on the same page of a notebook as the relevant census information, or may be cross-referenced to the notebook that has that information. It is best to record each subject's 'yes' or 'no' response as it is given, and not try to write down whether it is a positive or negative with regard to bilingual ability until after the interview is finished.

The questions should be put to the subjects in their mother tongue. This usually involves training a native speaker of the vernacular to administer the self-evaluation questionnaire. The person administering the self-evaluation questionnaire should have a clear idea of the point of each question and be able to elaborate on the question if the subject needs clarification. The same elaborations should be made each time clarification for that question is requested. A question which has been adequately contextualized and pilot tested normally contains within it all the necessary elaborations.

The questions on a self-evaluation questionnaire are generally asked in a particular order. Those questions thought to correspond with level one on the ILR skill level descriptions are asked first, then those thought to correspond to level two, and so on. Ideally the responses to a self-evaluation questionnaire are continuous. That is, all the answers to the lower-level questions are positive until a certain level is reached. After that, all the responses are negative.

It is important, however, to ask all of the questions on the self-evaluation questionnaire. Do not stop just because a subject gives several negative responses in a row. Responses to self-evaluation questionnaires are often discontinuous. It is not uncommon for subjects to give negative responses to questions intended to be at low levels and positive responses to questions intended to be at high levels. This situation occurs because the process of contextualizing a self-evaluation questionnaire is an imprecise one. When the contextualization is complete, it is not unusual for a question to now be more appropriate to a level other than that for which it was originally intended.[15]

Scoring a questionnaire. There are two ways of scoring the results of a self-evaluation questionnaire. If the results for each subject are fairly continuous, then the level at which the subject's responses to the questions change from positive to negative is the level of that person's bilingual ability. A subject must give a positive answer to every question at that level in order to have that assigned as the score. If the subject has not given a positive response to every question at that level, then the next lower level to which, the subject did give all positive responses is assigned. A 'plus' level is assigned to the base level if the subject has given positive responses to three of the questions at the next highest level. If the self-evaluation questionnaire has only three questions for each level, then it is not discriminatory enough for 'plus' levels to be assigned.

More often than not, however, the responses to self-evaluation questionnaires are discontinuous. If this is the case, it sometimes happens that the questions can be reordered so that they give a continuous set of responses for each subject. If this is the case, then it is acceptable to score the responses with the procedure outlined above on the basis of the new order.

If such reordering is not possible, the results for each self-evaluation questionnaire may be expressed in a variety of ways. For example, the percentage of questions to which positive responses are given may be calculated for each individual. These scores may then be tallied in the same way as scores on recorded text tests.

Alternatively, it is possible to look at the responses to the questionnaire as a whole. Even if the responses are discontinuous, it may be possible to note a decrease in positive responses to questions at the end of the questionnaire. Such a trend may not be immediately obvious. Should this be the case, the questionnaire responses are analyzed according the relevant social characteristics influencing bilingualism in the particular community being studied. The responses of educated people, for example might be separated from the responses of uneducated people. Then the percentage of positive responses given to each question by the portions of the sample is calculated in order to see if some questions are answered less positively by one part of the sample

---

[15]Indeed, there is some question whether the idea of assigning a particular language task to a particular level is not spurious.

than the same questions are answered by another portion of the sample. This indicates that one portion of the sample views itself as less bilingual than the other portion.

10.3 Advantages

An advantage of the type of questionnaire discussed in this chapter is that it can yield valuable information about language use patterns. When properly contextualized it provides a way of ranking respondants in terms of bilingual ability. Another advantage of self-evaluation questionnaires lies in their not taking long to administer. They provide a way to evaluate the bilingual competence of many individuals in a relatively short period of time.

10.4 Disadvantages

A disadvantage to self-evaluation questionnaires is common to questionnaires in general. Self-reported data tends to have problems in the areas of reliability and validity. With regard to self-evaluation questionnaires in particular, it is not uncommon for people to either overrate or underrate what they can do with language. As Khubchandani (1983) points out, language image (what one thinks one does with a language) and language posture (what one claims to be able to do with a language) often differ radically from language usage (what one actually does with a language.) This does not in itself make the responses to self-evaluation questionnaires uninteresting,[16] but it is doubtful that they are a direct measure of bilingual ability.

Another disadvantage to self-evaluation questionnaires is that translation and necessary contextualization of the questions sometimes ruins the correlation between a question and a particular level. If this results in a discontinuous series of responses to the questions, it can render the results very difficult to interpret. It seems to be necessary to calibrate discontinuous versions of a self-evaluation questionnaire against some other measure of bilingual ability in order to understand the results.[17] As Grimes (1986a) points out:

---

[16]For example, in some cases self-evaluation questionnaire may be a measure of desired bilingual ability. Desired bilingual ability may sometimes correlate with actual bilingual ability.

[17]Quakenbush (1986) describes how such a calibration might be accomplished.

> Questionnaires ask only for opinions; the results need to be verified ... by direct testing of actual proficiency and by observation.

A final problem with self-evaluation questionnaires is a result of the presuppositions that underlie the evaluation technique. The method appears to assume that there is a hierarchy of tasks that corresponds to different levels of bilingual ability. Being able to buy a bus ticket is taken as an indication that a person is level one; being able to interpret a speech by a local leader is taken as an indication that a person is level three or four. The assumption that certain tasks are easier to do in the second language than others is almost certainly incorrect. Even if it were correct, the hierarchy of tasks would probably vary from community to community. It seems much more realistic to say that people acquiring a second language can do a wide variety of tasks with various degrees of effectiveness. A person attempting to buy a bus ticket would be much more effective if she were at level two than if she were level one. But even a person at level two will sometimes fail to get a bus ticket—even educated mother-tongue speakers sometimes fail to get bus tickets!

11
Language Use and Language Attitudes

>High thoughts must have high language.
>
>Aristophanes
>*Frogs*

11.1 Introduction

Another goal of surveys is to investigate the patterns of language use in a community and the attitudes of that community towards their own language and towards other languages spoken in the region being surveyed. A study of language use seeks to describe the choices that people make about what speech varieties to use in particular situations. Such a study may also be interested in why individuals think a particular speech variety is more appropriate to a given situation and what the choices that are made say about cultural values. A survey which begins to investigate why a community considers certain speech varieties more appropriate to certain contexts has begun to study language attitudes. Specific attitudes towards different language varieties may openly acknowledged or tacitly understood; they may be widespread or idiosyncratic. Khubchandani (1983:40) reserves the term LANGUAGE USE to refer to what people may be observed actually doing with language. He distinguishes language use from language image. LANGUAGE IMAGE refers to what people think they do with the speech varieties they control (or think they control). Khubchandani further distinguishes both language use and language image from LANGUAGE POSTURE. Language posture is what people claim they do with the speech varieties they control (or think they control). This three-fold distinction should be kept in mind by researchers investigating language use and attitudes. Language images can be very hard to elicit unless one is fluent in the speech varieties used by the community being studied. In some cases it is even difficult to elicit language postures.

Oral varieties of language are not the only varieties of interest to a surveyor. In many cases it is important to investigate the use of various scripts which may be used to write. Attitudes towards different scripts may be influenced by the same sorts of factors which influence attitudes towards oral varieties.

Language use and language attitude studies are usually undertaken at the same time that a bilingualism study is carried out. If a community is fairly bilingual, such a study focuses on the relationship between a community's first and second languages. If a community is not bilingual, attitudes towards other related dialects are investigated. Attitudes towards related dialects are often worthy of investigation even in a bilingual community.

11.2 Language Use

Situations in which individuals find themselves often have a great influence on the speech variety they choose to use. These situations are often referred to as DOMAINS. A domain is an institutional context in which one language variety is more likely to be appropriate than another (Fasold 1984:183). Examples of various domains are family, friendship, neighborhood, school, work, government, and religion. When an individual speaks to another individual in the context of one of these domains, there is often a correlation between the domain and the speech variety used. The domains relevant to a survey vary from project to project.

Domains are not the only factor to affect language choice. An individual's perceptions of a situation also influence choice of speech variety. For example, Herman (1968:495–96) maintains that if speakers perceive a situation to be one in which their own interpersonal needs are in focus, their language choice may be different from what it might be if a task or a larger social group were in focus. In other words, speakers sometimes find themselves in overlapping domains, in each of which a different language variety would normally be used. In such cases a choice among possible language varieties needs to be made.

Herman discusses factors which are likely to influence language choice in such situations. He describes three psychological situations which commonly occur when domains overlap. He also educes the circumstances which characterize these situations. For example, a situation focused on interpersonal needs is more common when the setting is private rather than public. Similarly, a shared task is more likely to be the psychological focus of the speakers if the current behavior is task oriented. Fasold

Survey on a Shoestring 109

(1984:188) summarizes these situations and the cognitive circumstances which influence them in a chart similar to (33).

(33) Cognitive circumstances characteristic of psychological situations which influence language choice

Situation	Circumstances
Interpersonal interaction in focus	1. Setting is private rather than public. 2. Situation provokes insecurity, high tension, or frustration. 3. Situation deals with core rather than peripheral layers of personality.
Group identification in focus	1. Activity takes place in a public rather than a private setting. 2. Behavior in the situation may be interpreted as providing cues to group identifications. 3. Person involved in activity wishes to identify with particular group or be dissociated from it.
Shared task in focus	1. Person is not concerned about group identifications. 2. Behavior is task-oriented. 3. Well-established patterns of behavior characterize relationship.

Language use studies classify the speech varieties used by a community according to the domain in which they are used by members of the community. Exceptions to such classifications are often due to overlapping domains. In such instances, an understanding of the psychological situation in which the speakers find themselves will often provide clarification.

11.3 Language Attitudes

Language attitudes are the attitudes which a person holds towards the various speech varieties which are known to that individual. Language attitudes may be assessed as being on a continuum from positive to negative, as in (34).

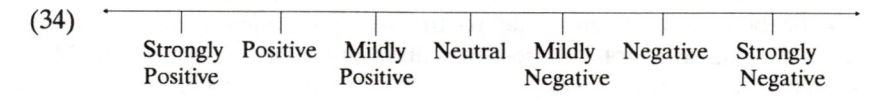

(34) Strongly Positive | Positive | Mildly Positive | Neutral | Mildly Negative | Negative | Strongly Negative

Language attitudes may be expressed both in terms of language image and language posture. A survey generally investigates only language posture because language images are rarely accessible to an outsider within the time span of a survey. Language image may vary widely from language posture, or it may be quite similar. Both are important, and the researcher should attempt to discover how similar image and posture are in any particular community.

11.4 Procedures

Language use and language attitudes have been an area of interest to sociolinguists since the inception of the discipline. Consequently many fine and ingenious methods of investigation have been devised for studying these phenomena. This discussion concentrates on three: MATCHED GUISE, OBSERVATION, and QUESTIONNAIRES.

Matched guise. Matched guise tests are an indirect method of eliciting information about language attitudes. Grosjean describes an ideal version of the matched guise test:

> ... perfectly bilingual speakers tape record a passage first in one of their languages and then in the other. The voices and the languages on the tape are randomized and then presented to judges who are asked to use the voice cues of the speakers to evaluate their personality characteristics: leadership, intelligence, character, kindness, and so on. The results show that the judges do not realize that the speakers are bilingual (1982:118).

Each speaker is represented by the same passage in two different languages, thus providing two 'guises' which are perfectly matched because they both come from the same speaker. If the 'judges' or test subjects react to the passage in one language consistently more favorably than they do to the passage in another language, it follows that their attitudes toward that language is more favorable. The use of two versions of the same passage spoken by the same speaker in two different languages provides a control on many of the variables that might otherwise have influenced the subjects.

Matched guise tests have been used as a technique to elicit information about language attitudes in literate societies for about thirty years. Various modifications have been made to the test methodology as a result of practical exigencies of different research situations. Only recently have attempts been made to adapt the method for use in preliterate societies.

Langan (1986) describes a matched guise test done in rural Guatemala. Showalter (to appear) describes the use of a matched guise test among the Kan people of Burkina Faso in which attitudes toward six different language varieties were elicited.

Observation. The use of observation as a technique for gathering bilingualism data is described above in chapter 10. The same techniques may be applied to collecting information about language use and language attitudes. The focus of the observations is different, but the skills required are the same. Observation is particularly useful in a language use and language attitudes study because a comparison of the findings from questionnaires with those derived from observation can show if there is a difference between language usage and language posture. If such a difference exists, this is an important clue in establishing whether or not language image differs significantly from language posture.

Observations relevant to language use and language attitudes should be recorded in a journal shortly after they are made. Pertinent quotes generated in the course of informal interviews should also be written down. These materials are useful in fleshing out the information gathered in the course of administering a questionnaire. A fellow who says, "Show me the son of a donkey who has stopped speaking Korku!" is expressing a positive attitude toward his own language much more forcefully than any number of statements like: "Eighty-nine percent of the sample expressed positive attitudes towards the continued use of their vernacular."

Questionnaires. The use of questionnaires in a sociolinguistic survey to investigate bilingualism has also been discussed in the previous chapter. Questionnaires may be administered formally, or, more commonly, as part of an informal conversation. It is often possible to cover most of the items on a language use and attitude questionnaire while taking a word list. If an investigation into language use and language attitudes involves the use of a questionnaire, it is important to ensure that an adequate sample is interviewed. As a rule of thumb, the sample used to assess bilingualism is satisfactory.

Language use and language attitude questionnaires differ from survey to survey according to the community being surveyed. Questions should be cast into the mother tongue of the community being interviewed. The researcher usually does not know, at the beginning of a survey, exactly which questions are to be included in the language use and language attitude questionnaire. During the first two survey journeys, as the researcher collects word lists and does dialect intelligibility testing, pilot language use and language attitude questions should be tried out. Some questions will be found useful, others will need modification, and still others will be discarded. When the researcher is relatively happy with the list of questions, actual administration of the questionnaire can begin.

Sample language use and language attitude questionnaires, contextualized to meet the needs of a particular survey, are presented in (35) and (36). In these questionnaires, Konda Dora and Valmiki are the names of local ethnic groups. Both groups have mother tongues which are different from the local language of wider communication, Oriya, and from the official language of the area, Telugu.

(35) Language Use Questions

1. How often do you speak Oriya? Daily, weekly, monthly, never?
2. How often do you speak Telugu? Daily, weekly, monthly, never?
3. What language do you speak to the merchants at the bazaar?
4. What language do you speak to the merchants at the stores?
5. When do you speak Oriya to Konda Dora?
6. Do you ever speak Telugu to Konda Dora?
7. What language do you speak to a Kotia person?
8. What language do you speak to a Valmiki person?
9. What language do you speak to a Telugu person?
10. What language do you speak to someone you do not know?
11. Are there any Konda Dora who cannot speak Konda? If yes, where?
12. Are there any Konda Dora who speak Konda differently from you? If yes, where?
13. What language will a Konda Dora specialist use to conduct a ritual?
14. If you want an Oriya specialist to perform a ritual for you, in what language do you discuss the matter (with him)?
15. What language will a Oriya specialist use to conduct a ritual ?
16. In what language(s) do you speak to your spouse?
17. In what language(s) does your spouse speak to you?
18. In what language(s) do you speak to your parents?
19. In what language(s) do your parents speak to you?
20. In what language(s) do you speak to your children?
21. In what language(s) do your children speak to you?
22. In what language(s) does your spouse speak to your children?
23. In what language(s) do your children speak to your spouse?
24. In what language(s) do you speak to your brother(s)?
25. In what language(s) do you speak to your sister(s)?

In addition to these questions, it is also necessary to have the appropriate census data for each individual in the sample.

As may be seen from the sample questionnaires, questions generally fall into two categories. One kind of question requires the person to give the name of a language as an answer; the other category requires a 'yes' or 'no' response. If language use patterns are fairly consistent throughout the

Survey on a Shoestring

(36) Language Attitude Questions
1. Should your children be able to speak Konda?
2. Should your children be able to speak Oriya?
3. Should your children be able to speak Telugu?
4. What language should a mother speak to her children?
5. What language do children learn to speak first?
6. What language do children learn to speak second?
7. What language do children learn to speak third?
8. What language would you like to know better?
9. There is one Oriya-medium and one Konda-medium school. To which school will you send your children?
10. There is one Telugu-medium and one Konda-medium school. To which school will you send your children?
11. There is one Oriya-medium and one Telugu-medium school. To which school will you send your children?
12. Should your children be able to read Konda?
13. Should your children be able to read Oriya?
14. Should your children be able to read Telugu?
15. Will you marry a woman who speaks only Oriya?
16. Will you marry a man who speaks only Oriya?
17. Will you marry a woman who speaks only Telugu?
18. Will you marry a man who speaks only Telugu?

sample, the data concerning language use may be presented in tabular form as in (37). Several such tables can be used to present information concerning different subsets of the sample if language use patterns are found to vary according to different social characteristics.

(37) Language Use in a Kannada Community

Language used:	Kannada	Tamil	Telugu
1. At home	x		
2. At market		x	x
3. At temple		x	
4. In worship[18]	x		
5. Within caste	x		
6. With relatives	x		
7. Between castes		x	x

Alternatively, if the data show a considerable degree of variance in the sample or subsets of the sample with reference to language use data, the

---

[18]This refers to those kinds of worship normally done at home or outside the context of a temple.

percentage of people in the sample who report using a particular language in a domain can be shown, as in (38).

(38) Hypothetical Language Use Pattern

Language used:	Mother Tongue	2nd Lg.	Both Lgs.
1. At home	65%	10%	25%
2. At market	5%	80%	15%
3. At temple		63%	37%
4. In worship	89%		11%
5. Within caste	76%	4%	20%
6. With Relatives	94%		6%
7. Between castes		100%	

Data generated by language attitude questions generally indicate either a positive or a negative attitude towards a particular language. Such data may also be presented in a table similar to that in (38). Depending on the percentage of the sample or subset of the sample expressing a positive or negative attitude towards a particular speech variety, the attitude of the population may be characterized according to the continuum in (34).

Language use and language attitude questionnaires are very good at eliciting information about language posture. They are limited in their ability to elicit information about language image, unless these two happen to be close to the same in the community being investigated. For this reason it is important that information elicited with a questionnaire be validated whenever possible with data from observation.

11.5 Summary

This chapter has looked at language use patterns as a function of the choices that individuals make about the speech varieties they use in specified contexts. Language use patterns should be studied according to the domains relevant to the community. Anomalous cases of language use are understood as the result of an overlap of domains. The cognitive perceptions of the individuals involved are recognized as an important factor influencing language choice in such cases.

Language attitudes have been discussed in this chapter as falling along a continuum ranging from strongly positive to strongly negative. It is important to distinguish between language image on the one hand and language posture on the other. This involves making some attempt to see whether language image and language posture are similar. Examining the difference between reported language use and observed language use is often helpful in this regard.

This chapter has also examined three ways of collecting information about language use and language attitudes: matched guise tests, observation, and questionnaires. These methods complement each other and should be used together whenever possible. Ways of presenting data gathered in the course of observations and interviews are discussed.

Appendix I
Storing Data on Computer

With the rapid expansion of memory capabilities in computers, many of the assumptions and conventions in this section already seem curiously dated. Laptops with built-in hard disks are available, making database programs like Shoebox (Wimbish 1990) attractive to the survey researcher in the field. Many of the following suggestions assume that the researcher is using a computer with little memory space (e.g., a Sharp PC-5000) in the analysis of data and the writing of the report. Consequently, the discussion that follows assumes a familiarity with a small-memory word processor like the Ed and Manuscripter programs developed by Jungle Aviation and Radio Service (JAARS). Therefore all the files described in this section use standard format conventions of the sort described in the documentation for the Direct Translator Support (DTS) software. This makes the recording of information and its organization into a specific format relatively standard.

A survey report on computer is composed of files with different contents and formats: text files, bibliography files, data files, questionnaire files, word list files, test files, etc. The contents of all of these are explained by the key files.

Text files

Text files contain the various drafts of the text of the survey report as it is being written.

File names and size. The first two or three characters can be used to indicate the language or ethnolinguistic group that the survey report is about, as in (39).

(39)   KDD1.1 = Konda Dora Report, chapter 1, first draft
         KR2.1 = Kurumba Report, chapter 2, first draft
         KM1.2 = Kolam Report, chapter 1, second draft
         KK1A.2 = Korku Report, chapter 1, part A, second draft
         KL7C.3 = Kullu Report, chapter 7, part C, third draft

A convenient three character code for each language may be drawn from *Ethnologue* (Grimes 1988b). The third or fourth character of the file name should be a number indicating which chapter of the report is contained in that file. The first character after the period should indicate which version of the file it is. A .1 is a first draft; a .2 file is a second draft.

It is recommended that files be kept shorter than 20K in size (i.e., about nine or ten pages, depending on the print format). If a single chapter is longer than 20K, the chapter number in the file name can be suffixed with a letter of the alphabet to show which part of the chapter it is. (These suggestions have been adapted from those in the File Management chapter of the documentation for the DTS software.)

File identification line and format. Each file should begin with an identification line. This line is always prefaced with a standard identification line marker: \id.

This line should contain: the file name, the name of the person responsible for the file, the date of the last edit, the title of the survey report and the chapter title. It may also describe which subsection of the chapter is in the file. The format in (40) is typical for the identification line.

(40)   \id KK2C.2, 870703, James Stahl, Korku Report, Goals

This identification line says that the file is second draft of the third part of the second chapter which addresses goals of the Korku report by James Stahl and that it was last edited on July 3, 1987.

The contents of files should be organized by standard format markers as described in the documentation for the consistent changes table that is being used to format the report. For an introduction to the concept of standard format markers, see the chapter by that name in the documentation for the DTS software.

Survey on a Shoestring 119

Bibliography files

Bibliography files contain a list of the written sources consulted in the course of the survey and the relevant information extracted from them. A bibliography file forms part of the final report and so is treated as one of the text files. The contents of files should be organized by standard format markers as described in the documentation for the consistent changes table that is being used to format the report.

Response files

These files contain the responses to the various questionnaires and tests used in the survey. Each file contains all the responses of a particular sample to a given questionnaire or test. The largest response file usually consists of the information from which the demographic profile is developed; it must often be broken into several files.

File names and size. The first two characters of the name of a response file should be RE to signify that it is a response file. This should be followed by two characters signifying which type of responses the file contains, as in (41).

(41)   REBLSEMA.KK = contains the bilingualism data for the Kaskor report for Semamata village
REDMWARS.LM = contains the demographic data for the Lamma report from Warshal village
RELUBEER.KR = contains the language use data for the Krantu report for Beeri village
RERTTEPA.KDD = contains the recorded text test data for the Komli Dado report for Pantsal village on the Telugu test
RESRNEBH.TMG = contains the sentence repetition test data for the Timog report for Bahansa on the Nemani test

For example, LU is used for language use questionnaires, LA for language attitudes, BL for bilingualism questionnaires, DM for demographic data collected through a census, 'RT' for recorded text test data, SR for sentence repetition test data. The remaining four letters of the file name specify the community from which the sample was drawn. In the case of recorded text and sentence repetition test data the fifth and sixth characters are used to specify the language or text which was tested and the seventh and eighth characters are used to specify the community. Response file names are suffixed after the period with the two or three letter designation which indicates the survey to which the file belongs. It is recommended that response files be kept under 20K in size. A response file longer than this can be broken into several files. A number can be substituted for the second character of the file name (i.e., the E in RE) to designate the sequence.

File identification line and format. Each response file begins with an identification line similar to that described for the text files. It should, however, briefly identify what kind of data is in the file rather than what chapter of the report.

Response files organize information with standard format markers. Each marker designates the response to one question on the questionnaire. For example, the response file for a ten-item questionnaire would have a marker for each question. In addition the file would have to specify who gave the particular responses by referring either by name or number to the person who gave the responses. A set of standard format markers is repeated for each member of the sample as in (42).

(42) \wh Shiva
\01 1
\02 0
\03 1
\04 0
\05 0
\06 1
\07 1
\08 1
\09 1
\10 0

In this set of standard format markers, \wh identifies the person who gave the responses. If a name is used to identify the responses, care should be taken that the name uniquely identifies an individual and that the key file identifies the response file in which the demographic information for that individual may be found. In this example, the marker \01 contains the response to question one, the marker \02 contains the response to question two, etc. The key file for that response file should also indicate which questionnaire or test file contains the questions to which the responses belong. In a response file, a zero is commonly used to represent a negative or incorrect response, and a one is used to represent a positive or correct response. Response files may also be used to keep track of nondigital responses, if so desired.

Word list files

Word list files contain the word lists elicited during a survey.

File names and size. Word list file names begin with WD; the rest of the file name is used to specify the language or dialect(s) the file contains word lists for. Like response files, word list files are suffixed with the two or three character code which identifies the survey to which the texts belong. When a word list file becomes too large to be conveniently edited as a single unit, it must be subdivided. (This threshold is usually reached around 30–35K.) For example, word list items 1–49 may be placed in a file called WD001.KDD; items 50–99 in file WD050.KDD; items 100–149 in WD100.KDD.

File identification line and format. Word list files should begin with an identification line. This line is similar to that described for text and response files, except that it identifies the languages of the word list in the file as well as the name of the person and community from which the word list was elicited.

Word lists are stored in standard format. Standard format codes like those in the example below are used. The initial sets of standard format markers are used for information about the word list. It is good to have a file which contains only the standard format codes for the numbers and glosses of the word list. This file serves as a template which can be replicated for each separate set of word lists to be entered. A set of standard format marker is repeated for each item in the word list.

(43) \num
 \gls LANGUAGE NAME
 \l01 Hindi
 \l02 Gujarati
 \l03 Urdu

\num
\gls DATE ELICITED
\101 January, 1986
\102 February, 1987
\103 April, 1985

\num
\gls LOCATION
\101 Delhi
\102 Ahmedabad
\103 Hyderabad

\num
\gls SOURCE
\101 Ramesh
\102 Arun
\103 Ali

\num 1
\gls body
\101 ʃerːr
\102 ʃerːr
\103 dʒism

\num 2
\gls head
\101 sɩr
\102 maṭhu
\103 sɩr

Storing word lists in this format is preferable to creating a separate file for each word list because it is a convenient one for analysis. If desired, however, an individual word list may be easily extracted from files formatted in this manner.

Test files

Test files contain the transcriptions and translation of the texts used in various tests used in the course of the survey.

Survey on a Shoestring

File names and size. Test file names begin with TS; the rest of the file name is used to specify which text it is. Like response files, test files are suffixed with the two or three character code which identifies the survey to which the tests belong. As a separate file is used for each test, test files are rarely larger than 20K in size.

File identification line and format. As with other files, each test file should begin with an identification line. This line is similar to that described for report and response files, except that it identifies the language and subject matter of the text as well as the name of the community and person from which the text was elicited. Test files are for the texts used in recorded text testing. Each test file contains a single text. Test files contain three or four lines of material for each line of the text. Each line is introduced by \n, which designates the number of the line in the text. The line of text marked \p is a phonetic transcription of a sentence of the text. Another of these lines, marked \g, contains a gloss for each word in the line of text. This constitutes a word-for-word translation of the sentence. Still another line, marked \f, is an idiomatic translation of the text. If a transcription of the text in the script of the language is available, this might constitute still another line of the test file. Each of these lines, together with the number of the line of text is organized into a set of standard format markers, as in (44).

(44) \n 1
 \d ऐले हिन्न सक्दैन
 \p aile hin:ʌ sʌkdainʌ
 \g now walk-to cannot
 \f She can't walk yet.

These texts are entered in such a way that they may be printed interlinearly.

Questionnaire files

Questionnaire files contain copies of the various questionnaires used in the survey and their translations into the relevant languages. File names for questionnaires begin with QS, otherwise the file naming and identification conventions are identical to that of test files.

Some questionnaire files contain copies of the questions used for recorded text testing. The file naming and identification line conventions of these files follow those of response files. All questions for questionnaire files are entered with the same standard format markers used for text in text files.

Key files

Key files indicate the contents of the various other files. In particular key files contain a list of all the standard format markers used and what they mark. A key file also serves as a cross-reference between files. For example, if a particular response file contains several individuals' responses to questionnaires and does not include the relevant demographic information about those individuals, the key file should indicate which demographic file contains the needed information. (Some of this information should also be provided in the identification line of the file.) The name of a key file begins with KEY and is suffixed with the two or three character designation of the language group, as described above.

Appendix II
Survey Journeys

Many surveys seek to discover the existence of various dialect areas, the extent of bilingualism in those dialect areas, and the language use and attitude situations both within and among the various dialect areas. This appendix is intended to provide a practical example of how these various goals might be organized within the framework of a single survey. For the sake of this example a survey may be conceived of as a sequence of three discrete journeys to the various reference points. In principle, each of the reference points is visited once before any is visited a second time; each is visited a second time before any is visited a third time. The first two journeys are primarily concerned with identifying dialect areas; these journeys basically correspond to those described in Casad (1974:8–29). The third journey is mostly concerned with language attitudes, language use, and bilingualism.[19] In principle, the objectives of one journey are accomplished before moving on to the next journey. After each journey, the list of reference points is modified according to the data uncovered on that journey. Note that it may take several trips to a single reference point to accomplish the objectives described for any one journey.

---

[19]This distribution of objectives to different survey journeys, like other principles mentioned in this section, is intended only as an example, albeit one which has been found to be helpful. It is not always possible nor even neccesarily desirable to adhere to such guidelines strictly.

First journey

Once the initial list of reference points has been decided upon, the collection of data can begin. It usually requires two journeys to each reference point to acquire the data necessary for a survey of the dialect areas in that region.

Three objectives are to be accomplished on the first journey to any reference point. The first is to collect a word list which represents the dialect spoken at that reference point. This word list is thoroughly checked (i.e., elicit each item from more than one speaker) before leaving the community. The second objective is to collect an equally representative text suitable for use in dialect intelligibility testing. This text is transcribed, translated, and pilot tested on the first journey. The third objective is to hold a number of informal interviews with the inhabitants of the community and develop a brief description of the reference point. This description should include such things as a population, number of ethnolinguistic groups, physical and social amenities available (e.g., schools, electricity, water, health services, transportation), as well as information about surrounding communities and other languages spoken in the region.

The amount of time it takes to accomplish these three objectives varies from community to community. It is very difficult to complete these tasks in less than two days. If these three tasks cannot be completed within a week, then it is usually worthwhile to move on and select an equivalent community as a reference point.

When the first journey has been made to all the reference points, a preliminary analysis of the word lists is done. In particular the word lists are checked for synonyms and near synonyms. The variant forms for the different words on the word list are noted and a rough calculation of the degree of linguistic similarity indicated by the word lists is made. On the basis of word list data and interviews, additions to, and deletions from the list of reference points may be made. For example, if word lists from two reference points prove to be 96-percent similar and the informal interviews show that there is a large degree of integration between the two communities (e.g., people from the two communities routinely marry into the other community), it may be concluded that the dialects are substantially the same and one of the communities may be dropped from the list of reference points. Similarly, information discovered during the first survey journey may point to the existence of a previously unsuspected dialect. This would require that a community using that dialect be added to the list of reference points.

Second journey

Once the list of reference points has been revised to take into account the information discovered on the first survey journey, it is time to make a second journey to the various reference points.[20] The primary objective of the second journey is to test the various texts collected on the first journey in communities other than those in which they were collected. All of the texts used in dialect intelligibility testing must first be tested and validated in the communities where they were collected. This is done during the first journey. On the second journey dialect intelligibility testing is completed by testing the texts in other communities in order to see how well they are understood.

Another objective of the second journey is to recheck the word list. The word lists collected on the first journey invariably contain words which, while common to the dialect area, were only elicited at one reference point. These words are usually near synonyms to the words elicited at the other reference points. The preliminary analysis completed after the first survey journey is designed to spot such words. For example, 'rock' and 'stone' are both commonly used as near synonyms in American English. A word list elicited in one place may include 'rock', while in another 'stone' may be included. When such sets including multiple words for a particular item on the word list are elicited, it is necessary to check whether or not the alternate words are also known and used. This can be done to some extent even on the first journey, but usually must also be carried over to the second journey as well.

Another objective of the second journey to the various reference points often is to do some pilot testing of bilingual ability using recorded text tests. Such pilot testing is done on a much smaller scale than a rigorous investigation into bilingualism, but helps to give some idea of where it might be necessary to do more extensive bilingualism investigations. Such pilot testing may also be done on the first journey. On the second journey, as well as the first, it is a good idea to collect descriptive information through informal interviews with the people living at the various reference points.

The amount of time it takes to complete the objectives of the second journey at a particular reference point varies between two days and a week. It depends on how many texts must be tested and how readily people listen to the texts. When the second journey to the reference points

---

[20]If a community has been added to the list of reference points it is a good idea to visit it and complete the objectives mentioned for the first journey before proceeding with plans for the second journey.

has been completed, an analysis of the word lists and dialect intelligibility data collected should yield a fairly comprehensive picture of the dialect areas in the region being surveyed.

Third journey

When the number of dialect areas has been identified, it is possible to start with the third part of the survey—an investigation into bilingualism, language use, and language attitudes. The list of reference points is narrowed to include only one or two communities in each language area. At these points an extensive investigation into language use, language attitudes, and bilingualism is carried out. If at all possible, the researcher should arrange to live in these communities while the study is underway.

For each of these reference points, it takes three to four weeks to complete the necessary investigations. The first half of the time is spent developing and analyzing a demographic profile of the community in order to apply the tests to a representative sample of the community's population. The second half of the time is spent actually doing the various procedures used in the study to measure bilingual ability, language use, and language attitudes.

References
and a selection of collateral readings

Adams, Marianne Lehr and James R. Frith, eds. 1979. Testing kit (French and Spanish). Washington: U.S. Department of State.

Agheyisi, Rebecca and Joshua Fishman. 1970. Language attitude studies: a brief survey of methodological approaches. Anthropological Linguistics 12(5):137–57.

Bailey, Thomas Grahame. 1908. Languages of the northern Himalayas. London: Royal Asiatic Society.

Blair, Frank 1986a. A sociolinguistic profile of Kullu district, Himachal Pradesh. Unpublished manuscript.

———. 1986b. A sociolinguistic profile of Kurumba dialects. Unpublished manuscript.

Brewster, E. Thomas and Elizabeth S. Brewster. 1976. Language acquisition made practical. Oakland: Lingua House.

Casad, Eugene. 1974. Dialect intelligibility testing. Summer Institute of Linguistics Publications in Linguistics and Related Fields 38. Norman, Oklahoma: The Summer Institute of Linguistics and the University of Oklahoma.

Christian, Donna. 1989. Language planning: the view from linguistics. In F. Newmeyer (ed.), Linguistics: the Cambridge survey, 193–209. Vol. 4, Language: the socio-cultural context. Cambridge: Cambridge University Press.

Eastman, Carol M. 1983. Language planning: an introduction. San Francisco: Chandler & Sharp.

El-Dash, Linda G. and G. Richard Tucker. 1976. Subjective reactions to various speech styles in Egypt. International Journal of the Sociology of Language 6:33–54.

Fasold, Ralph. 1984. The sociolinguistics of society. Language and Society 5. Oxford: Basil Blackwell.

Fishman, Joshua A. Who speaks what language to whom and when. La Linguistique 2:67–88.

Grimes, Barbara F. 1985. Comprehension and language attitudes in relation to language choice for literature and education in preliterate societies. Journal of Multilingual and Multicultural Development 6(2):165–81.

———. 1986a. Evaluating bilingual proficiency in language groups for cross-cultural communication. Notes on Linguistics. 33:5–27.

———. 1986b. Language skills required of a disciple. Notes on Scripture in Use 9:19–23.

———. 1986c. Regional and other nonstandard dialects of major languages. Notes on Linguistics. 35:19–39.

———. 1988a. Why test intelligibility? Notes on Linguistics. 42:39–64.

———, ed. 1988b. The ethnologue: Languages of the world. 11th edition. Dallas: Summer Institute of Linguistics.

Grimes, Joseph E. 1988. Correlations between vocabulary similarity and intelligibility. Notes on Linguistics 41:19–33.

Grosjean, François. 1982. Life with two languages: an introduction to bilingualism. Cambridge: Harvard University Press.

Hari, Anna Maria, ed. 1971. Conversational Nepali. Kathmandu, Nepal: Summer Institute of Linguistics Institute of Nepal Studies, Tribhuvan University.

Herman, Simon. 1968. Explorations in the social psychology of language choice. In Joshua A. Fishman (ed.), Readings in the sociology of language, 492–511. The Hague: Mouton.

Jones, Randall L. 1975. Testing language proficiency in the United States Government. In Randall L. Jones and Bernard Spolsky (eds.), Testing Language Proficiency, 1–9. Washington: Center for Applied Linguistics.

——— and Bernard Spolsky, eds. 1975. Testing language proficiency. Washington: Center for Applied Linguistics.

Keesing, Roger M. 1973. Kwara?ae ethnoglottochronology: procedures used by Malaita cannibals for determining percentages of shared cognates. American Anthropologist 75:1282–89.

Keller, Barbara L. 1986. A qualitative approach to the study of language and identity in Ladakh. M.A. Thesis. University of Texas at Arlington.

Khubchandani, Lachman M. 1978. Distribution of contact languages in India: a study of the 1961 bilingualism returns. In Joshua A. Fishman, ed., Advances in the study of societal multilingualism, 553–86. The Hague: Mouton.

———. 1983. Plural languages, plural cultures. Hawaii: University of Hawaii Press.

Lado, Robert. 1978. Scope and limitations of interview-based language testing: are we asking too much of the interview. In John L. D. Clark, ed., Direct Testing of Speaking Proficiency: theory and application, 113–28. Princeton, New Jersey: Educational Testing Service.

Langan, Katherine A. 1986. Language attitude testing of a preliterate ethnolinguistic minority. M.A. Thesis. Georgetown University.

Lantolf, James P. and Willam Frawley. 1985. Oral-proficiency testing: a critical analysis. The Modern Language Journal 69(4):337–45.

Lehmann, Winifred P. 1973. Historical linguistics: an introduction. Second edition. New York: Holt, Rinehart and Winston.

Marshall, David. 1986. A sociolinguistic survey of Koya dialects. Unpublished manuscript.

Norman, Donald A. 1976. Memory and attention. New York: John Wiley and Sons.

Platt, Jennifer. 1983. The development of the 'participant observation' method in sociology: origin, myth, and history. Journal of the History of the Behavioral Sciences 19(4):379–93.

Quakenbush, John Stephen. 1986. Language use and proficiency in a multilingual setting: a sociolinguistic survey of Agutaynen speakers in Palawan, Philippines. Ph.D. Dissertation. Georgetown University.

Radloff, Carla. To appear. Sentence repetition for bilingualism testing: field test report and methodology. In Gloria E. Kindell (ed.), Bilingualism:

Papers from the 1987 Asia Area Survey Conference. Dallas: Summer Institute of Linguistics.

Radloff, Carla and David Marshall. 1986. Sentence repetition: a pilot study. Unpublished manuscript.

Rubin, Joan. 1971. Evaluation and language planning. In Rubin and Jernudd 1971, 217–52. Also in Fishman 1972, 476–510.

——— and Bjorn Jernudd, eds. 1971. Can languages be planned? Honolulu: University Press of Hawaii.

Saussure, Ferdinand de. 1959. A course in general linguistics. Charles Bally and Albert Sechehaye, eds. New York: Philosophical Library.

Savignon, Sandra J. 1985. Evaluation of communicative competence: the ACTFL provisional proficiency guidelines. The Modern Language Journal. 69(2):129–34.

Showalter, Stuart D. To appear. Using indirect methods for a language attitude survey of a dialect chain in rural Burkina Faso. In Gloria E. Kindell (ed.), Proceedings of the International Language Assessment Conference. Dallas: Summer Institute of Linguistics.

Simons, Gary F. 1983. Language variation and the limits to communication. Dallas, Texas: Summer Institute of Linguistics.

———. 1984. Word list analysis in the field with a notebook computer. Occasional Publications in Academic Computing 5. Dallas, Texas: Summer Institute of Linguistics.

Sollenberger, Howard E. 1978. Development and current use of the FSI oral interview test. In John L. D. Clark (ed.), Direct Testing of Speaking Proficiency: theory and application, 1–12. Princeton, New Jersey: Educational Testing Service.

Spradley, James P. 1979. The ethnographic interview. New York: Holt, Rinehart and Winston.

———. 1980. Participant observation. New York: Holt, Rinehart and Winston.

Stahl, James L. 1986. A sociolinguistic survey of the Korku language area. Unpublished manuscript.

Summer Institute of Linguistics. 1987. Second language oral proficiency evaluation. Notes on Linguistics 40:24–54.

Wilds, Claudia P. 1975. The oral interview test. In Randall L. Jones and Bernard Spolsky (eds), Testing Language Proficiency, 29–44. Washington. Center for Applied Linguistics.

Wimbish, John S. 1989. Wordsurv: a program for analyzing language survey word lists. Occasional Notes in Academic Computing 13. Dallas: Summer Institute of Linguistics.

———. 1990. Shoebox: a data management program for the field linguist. Version 1.2. Ambon, Indonesia: Summer Institute of Linguistics and Pattimura University.

Summer Institute of Linguistics and The University of Texas at Arlington Publications in Linguistics

(* = in microfiche only)

1. **Comanche Texts** by E. Canonge (1958) *
2. **Pocomchi Texts** by M. Mayers (1958) *
3. **Mixteco Texts** by A. Dyk (1959) *
4. **A Synopsis of English Syntax** by E. A. Nida (1960) *
5. **Mayan Studies I** by W. C. Townsend et al. (1960) *
6. **Sayula Popoluca Texts, with Grammatical Outline** by L. Clark (1961) *
7. **Studies in Ecuadorian Indian Languages: I** by C. Peeke et al. (1962) *
8. **Totontepec Mixe Phonotagmemics** by J. C. Crawford (1963) *
9. **Studies in Peruvian Indian Languages: I** by M. Larson et al. (1963) *
10. **Verb Studies in Five New Guinea Languages** by A. Pence et al. (1964)
11. **Some Aspects of the Lexical Structure of a Mazatec Historical Text** by G. M. Cowan (1965) *
12. **Chatino Syntax** by K. Pride (1965) *
13. **Chol Texts on the Supernatural** by A. Whittaker and V. Warkentin (1965) *
14. **Phonemic Systems of Colombian Languages** by V. G. Waterhouse et al. (1967) *
15. **Bolivian Indian Tribes: Classification, Bibliography and Map of Present Language Distribution** by H. and M. Key (1967)
16. **Bolivian Indian Grammars, I and II** by E. Matteson et al. (1967) *
17. **Totonac: from Clause to Discourse** by A. Reid et al. (1968) *
18. **Tzotzil Grammar** by M. M. Cowan (1969)
19. **Aztec Studies I: Phonological and Grammatical Studies in Modern Nahuatl Dialects** by D. F. Robinson et al. (1969)
20. **The Phonology of Capanahua and its Grammatical Basis** by E. E. Loos (1969)
21. **Philippine Languages: Discourse, Paragraph and Sentence Structure** by R. E. Longacre (1970)
22. **Aztec Studies II: Sierra Nahuat Word Structure** by D. F. Robinson (1970)
23. **Tagmemic and Matrix Linguistics Applied to Selected African Languages** by K. L. Pike (1970)
24. **A Grammar of Lamani** by R. L. Trail (1970)
25. **A Linguistic Sketch of Jicaltepec Mixtec** by C. H. Bradley (1970)
26. **Major Grammatical Patterns of Western Bukidnon Manobo** by R. E. Elkins (1970)
27. **Central Bontoc: Sentence, Paragraph and Discourse** by L. A. Reid (1970)
28. **Identification of Participants in Discourse: A Study of Aspects of Form and Meaning in Nomatsiguenga** by M. R. Wise (1971)
29. **Tupi Studies I** by D. Bendor-Samuel et al. (1971)
30. **L'Enonce Toura (Côte d'Ivoire)** by T. Bearth (1971)
31. **Instrumental Articulatory Phonetics: An Introduction to Techniques and Results** by K. C. Keller (1971) *
32. **According to Our Ancestors: Folk Texts from Guatemala and Honduras** by M. Shaw et al. (1971) *

33. **Two Studies on the Lacandones of Mexico** by P. Baer and W. R. Merrifield (1971)
34. **Toward a Generative Grammar of Blackfoot** by D. G. Frantz (1971) *
35. **Languages of the Guianas** by J. E. Grimes et al. (1972) *
36. **Tagmeme Sequences in the English Noun Phrase** by P. Fries (1972)
37. **Hierarchical Structures in Guajajara** by D. Bendor-Samuel (1972)
38. **Dialect Intelligibility Testing** by E. Casad (1974)
39. **Preliminary Grammar of Auca** by M. C. Peeke (1973)
40. **Clause, Sentence, and Discourse Patterns in Selected Languages of Nepal**, parts I, II, III, IV by A. Hale et al. (1973)
41. **Patterns in Clause, Sentence, and Discourse in Selected Languages of India and Nepal**, parts I, II, III, IV by R. L. Trail et al. (1973)
42. **A Generative Syntax of Peñoles Mixtec** by J. Daly (1973)
43. **Daga Grammar** by E. Murane (1974)
44. **A Hierarchical Sketch of Mixe as spoken in San José El Paraíso** by W. and J. Van Haitsma (1976)
45. **Network Grammars** by J. E. Grimes et al. (1975) *
46. **A Description of Hiligaynon Syntax** by E. Wolfenden (1975)
47. **A Grammar of Izi, an Igbo Language** by P. and I. Meier and J. Bendor-Samuel (1975)
48. **Semantic Relationships of Gahuku Verbs** by E. Deibler (1976)
49. **Sememic and Grammatical Structures in Gurung** by W. Glover (1974)
50. **Korean Clause Structure** by Shin Ja Joo Hwang (1976)
51. **Papers on Discourse** by J. E. Grimes et al. (1978)
52. **Discourse Grammar: Studies in Indigenous Languages of Colombia, Panama, and Ecuador**, parts I, II, III by R. E. Longacre et al. (1976-77)
53. **Grammatical Analysis** by K. L. and E. G. Pike (1980; revised 1982); **Instructor's Guide for Grammatical Analysis** by K. L. and E. G. Pike (1976)
54. **Studies in Otomanguean Phonology** by W. R. Merrifield et al. (1977)
55. **Two Studies in Middle American Comparative Linguistics** by D. Oltrogge and C. Rensch (1977)
56. **Studies in Uto-Aztecan Grammar,** volumes I, II, III, IV by R. W. Langacker et al. (1977–84)
57. **The Deep Structure of the Sentence in Sara-Ngambay Dialogues** by J. E. Thayer (1978)
58. **Discourse Studies in Mesoamerican Languages,** parts I and II by L. K. Jones et al. (1979)
59. **The Functions of Reported Speech in Discourse** by M. L. Larson (1978)
60. **A Grammatical Description of the Engenni Language** by E. Thomas (1978)
61. **Predicate and Argument in Rengao Grammar** by K. Gregerson (1979)
62. **Nung Grammar** by J. E. Saul and N. F. Wilson (1980)
63. **Discourse Grammar in Ga'dang** by M. R. Walrod (1979)
64. **A Framework for Discourse Analysis** by W. Pickering (1980)
65. **A Generative Grammar of Afar** by L. Bliese (1981)
66. **The Phonology and Morphology of Axininca Campa** by D. L. Payne (1981)
67. **Pragmatic Aspects of English Text Structure** by L. B. Jones (1983)
68. **Syntactic Change and Syntactic Reconstruction** by J. R. Costello (1983)
69. **Affix Positions and Cooccurrences** by J. E. Grimes (1983)

70. **Babine and Carrier Phonology: A Historically Oriented Study** by G. Story (1984)
71. **Workbook for Historical Linguistics** by W. P. Lehmann (1984)
72. **Senoufo Phonology, Discourse to Syllable** by E. Mills (1984)
73. **Pragmatics in Non-Western Perspective** by G. L. Huttar and K. J. Gregerson (1986)
74. **English Phonetic Transcription** by Ch.-J. N. Bailey (1985)
75. **Sentence Initial Devices** by J. E. Grimes et al. (1986)
76. **Hixkaryana and Linguistic Typology** by D. C. Derbyshire (1985)
77. **Discourse Features of Korean Narration** by S. J. Hwang (1987)
78. **Tense/Aspect and the Development of Auxiliaries in Kru Languages** by L. Marchese (1986)
79. **Modes in Dényá Discourse** by S. N. Abangma (1987)
80. **Current Trends and Issues in Hispanic Linguistics** by L. Studerus (1987)
81. **Aspects of Western Subanon Formal Speech** by W. Hall (1987)
82. **Dinka Vowel System** by J. Malou (1988)
83. **Studies in the Syntax of Mixtecan Languages, volume I** by C. H. Bradley and B. E. Hollenbach (1988)
84. **Insights into Tagalog Reduplication, Infixation, and Stress from Nonlinear Phonology** by K. M. French (1988)
85. **The Verbal Piece in Ebira** by J. Adive (1989)
86. **Comparative Kadai: Linguistic Studies Beyond Tai** by J. Edmondson and D. Solnit (1988)
87. **An Etymological Dictionary of the Chinantec Languages: Studies in Chinantec Languages 1** by C. R. Rensch (1989)
88. **Lealao Chinantec Syntax: Studies in Chinantec Languages 2** by J. E. Rupp (1989)
89. **Comaltepec Chinantec Syntax: Studies in Chinantec Languages 3** by J. L. Anderson (1989)
90. **Studies in the Syntax of Mixtecan Languages 2** by C. H. Bradley and B. E. Hollenbach (1990)
91. **Language Maintenance in Melanesia: Sociolinguistics and Social Networks in New Caledonia** by Stephen Schooling (1990)
92. **Comanche Dictionary and Grammar** by L. W. Robinson and J. Armagost (1990)
93. **Development and Diversity: Language Variation across Time and Space—A Festschrift for Charles-James N. Bailey** by J. A. Edmondson, C. Feagin, and P. Mühlhäusler (1990)
94. **Ika Syntax: Studies in the Languages of Colombia 1** by P. Frank (1990)
95. **Syllables, Tone, and Verb Paradigms: Studies in Chinantec Languages 4** by W. R. Merrifield and C. R. Rensch (1990)
96. **Survey on a Shoestring: A Manual for Small-Scale Language Surveys** by Frank Blair (1990)

For further information or a catalog of all S.I.L. publications write to:

International Academic Bookstore
Summer Institute of Linguistics
7500 W. Camp Wisdom Road
Dallas, TX 75236